Profit from Your Platform:

Inside The Speaker's Revenue Streams

Profit from Your Platform:

Inside The Speaker's Revenue Streams

Copyright © 2025 Vincent Phipps
All rights reserved

Edited & Formatted by SayThat Publishing

Dedication

To all of my PSK'ers
Graduates of the 3-Day Masterclass:
Professional Speaker's Kit

Thank you

Thank you to all of the people who find value in learning new strategies to solve problems.

Table of Contents

Introduction: Your Journey to Professional Speaking......1
Chapter 1: The Business Fundamentals............................... 5
Chapter 2: Your Speaking Foundation................................41
Chapter 3: Crafting Your Speaking Topics & Content....81
Chapter 4: Finding Speaking Opportunities................... 131
Chapter 5: The Application Process................................. 177
Chapter 6: Working with Event Planners........................ 221
Appendix A: Speaker Application Checklist...................267
Appendix B: Sample Topic Titles and Descriptions....297
Appendix C: Learning Objectives Template................... 323
Appendix D: Professional Bio Templates........................331

Introduction: Your Journey to Professional Speaking

Welcome, future speaking superstar! Whether you're an aspiring or seasoned speaker looking to combine your passion with your presentations and impact a lot of people or you want to make more money to feed your lifestyle – you're reading the right book. You're exactly where you need to be.

I've been in the speaking industry since 1996. I've delivered thousands of presentations and faced nearly every challenge imaginable. Despite the hurdles, I've learned the keys to building a successful speaking business—one that not only engages and inspires audiences but also generates multiple revenue streams. In this book, I'll share all the insights I've gathered, giving you the tools to build your own successful career.

Embarking on a career in professional speaking is more than just stepping onto a platform and talking. It's about:

- Making a meaningful impact on people's lives
- Sharing your unique insights and experiences
- Creating a business that thrives on your passion
- Developing diverse income sources rooted in your expertise
- Enjoying the freedom to select projects and clients that excite and challenge you

Success in the speaking world demands more than excellent oratory skills. It requires:

- A compelling message that addresses real-world issues
- Professional-grade business practices and promotional materials
- Effective negotiation and pricing strategies
- Strong relationship-building skills to grow and maintain your network

- Persistence and resilience to overcome challenges and setbacks

There are five types of speakers (S.P.E.A.K.):

Starter

Promising

Expert

Awesome

King or Queen

Most paid speakers are in E, A, or K. No matter where you find yourself in the SPEAK categories, this book was written to help you along your journey.

Phipps Tip: One of the best ways to secure speaking engagements is to be seen in action. Initially, you may need to create opportunities for yourself. Focus on gaining exposure, delivering exceptional value, and captivating audiences wherever you can.

Chapter 1: The Business Fundamentals

Setting Up Your Speaking Business

To establish yourself as a professional speaker, it's essential to set up a solid business foundation from the start. Here's a practical guide to get you up and running:

Business Structure

- **Choose a business entity**: Options include LLC, sole proprietorship, etc., each with different implications for liability and taxes
- **Employer Identification Number (EIN)**: Necessary for tax purposes and to differentiate personal and business finances

- **Business bank account**: Essential for managing your finances professionally
- **Tracking system for income and expenses**: Keeps your financials organized and simplifies tax filing

Professional Tools

- **Business email and phone**: Establishes your professional presence and helps manage communication effectively
- **Business cards**: Useful for networking and leaving a tangible reminder of your services
- **Basic accounting software**: Streamlines financial management
- **CRM system**: Essential for maintaining relationships with clients and scheduling follow-ups

---

Phipps Tip: Identify the top 3 business systems you need *now*. For example, this may include an EIN, an accounting system, and a CRM.

Creating Your Brand

Building a compelling brand is about *more than just a logo*; it encompasses the entire presentation of yourself to the professional world.

Your Core Message

- **Identify the problems you solve**: Be clear about the issues your speech addresses
- **Target audience**: Understand who needs your solutions and tailor your message to them
- **Unique selling proposition**: Why should someone choose you over others?

Visual Identity

- **Professional headshots**: Portrays a professional image
- **Logo and color scheme**: Creates a visual identity that is memorable and appealing
- **Website and presentation templates**: Ensures consistency across all platforms

Brand Voice

- **Speaking style**: Should be consistent with your brand personality
- **Written communication**: Reflects your professional image, from emails to social media posts

> **Phipps Tip:** Keep your branding consistent but flexible enough to evolve with your career.

Learning from Mistakes

A personal anecdote can illustrate the importance of specificity in your branding. For example, early in my career, I described myself too generically as a "motivational speaker." A pivotal conversation with an event planner highlighted the need for specificity. She likened it to a restaurant vaguely claiming they "serve food" without specifying the type of cuisine, which doesn't entice a specific customer base.

Be Specific with Your Branding:

- Instead of saying "I'm a leadership speaker," specify "I help new managers at tech companies enhance their leadership skills for remote team management."
- Instead of "I speak about success," I detail "I guide entrepreneurs to scale their businesses from six figures to seven through strategic growth."

Real-World Pricing Examples

Share a story about the importance of strategic pricing and building relationships, like getting booked for a seemingly low fee but leveraging it into more lucrative engagements through referrals, illustrating the long-term benefits of strategic pricing and networking.

Revenue Streams in Action

Demonstrate the potential of diversifying income through:

- **Speaking fees**: Your primary income
- **Product sales**: Supplement your speaking fees by selling your products at events
- **Online courses**: Offer in-depth virtual learning options
- **Consulting**: Provide personalized follow-up services for deeper engagement

Example: One successful speaking engagement could include a $5,000 speaking fee, $2,500 from book sales, a $497 online course offering, and $2,000 from follow-up consulting, cumulatively surpassing $10,000.

This section outlines practical steps to setting up and branding your speaking business, leveraging personal stories for relatability, and illustrating effective strategies for maximizing revenue streams.

The Power of Positioning

One of the most insightful lessons about value perception comes from an unlikely source—rapper and entrepreneur "50 Cent" (Curtis Jackson). He once illustrated the concept of positioning using the simple example of a bottle of water:

- **At a grocery store**, the water might sell for $1.
- **At a sporting event**, the same bottle could go for $3.
- **In an airport**, it might be priced at $6.
- **In a desert**, it becomes **priceless**.

The water itself hasn't changed; the perceived value of the water caused the price to change.

As professional speakers, the lesson here is critical: **positioning is everything**. Your skills as a speaker—your voice, your message, your delivery—remain constant, but the value you provide can vary dramatically based on where and how you present it. Here's how you can apply this concept to enhance your speaking career:

Identify High-Value Opportunities

- Look for speaking opportunities where your message will be most impactful and valued. This could mean targeting industry conferences over general business gatherings, or specialized seminars where your expertise aligns closely with audience needs.

Tailor Your Offerings

- Adapt your talks for different audiences to increase relevance and perceived value. The more directly your message addresses the specific problems or aspirations of an audience, the more they are willing to invest in hearing it.

Leverage Scarcity

- Position yourself as a unique provider of your insights. This doesn't just mean claiming to be one-of-a-kind; it means clearly articulating what sets you apart from other speakers in your niche.

Optimize Your Pricing Strategy

- Just as the water bottle's price varies by location, consider varying your speaking fees based on the prestige of the event, the economic scale of the industry, or the budgetary norms of the region.

Strategic Marketing

- Market yourself in ways that highlight the unique benefits of your talks, especially through testimonials, case studies, and visible partnerships that attest to your value.

> **Phipps Tip:** Always remember that your core product—your speech—doesn't change much, but how and where you sell it can dramatically affect how much it's worth. Like 50 Cent's example, find your 'desert' where your speaking is indispensable and, therefore, highly valued.

This approach not only helps in maximizing your earnings but also in finding the most rewarding stages for your career. By understanding and implementing effective positioning, you set the stage for greater success and sustainability in the competitive world of professional speaking.

Real Speaker Business Tools

In the speaking business, effective management of leads and communications can significantly streamline your operations and enhance your professionalism. Here's a practical guide to the tools I use in my business to manage relationships and organize my workflow efficiently:

CRM Systems

When evaluating Contact Resource Manager (CRM) systems, especially for professional speakers who need to manage numerous client interactions and speaking engagements efficiently, here are some key features to consider:

- **Robust Search Engines**: Your CRM should offer advanced search capabilities that allow you to quickly navigate through vast amounts of data, including contact details, past conversations, communication histories, and next step requirements.
- **Automated Scheduling**: Look for a CRM that can automate reminders for follow-ups with potential leads or ongoing clients, helping you maintain timely interactions without missing key opportunities.
- **AI intervention:** Some CRMs integrate AI to suggest content for emails and proposals, tailored to each contact's history and preferences, enhancing personalization and effectiveness in communication.

- **Quality stipulations:** A useful feature is the ability to prioritize opportunities based on potential speaker fees and the strategic impact of each engagement, helping you focus on the most valuable prospects.
- **Organizational systems:** The CRM should enable a comprehensive listing of engagements by name, contact person, location, and other relevant details, making it easier to manage potential speaking opportunities, past presentations, and upcoming speaking events.

> **Phipps Tip:** Start with what you have and what you can afford. In the beginning, I used a simple Excel spreadsheet to manage my contacts and engagements. The key is to maintain organization from the start, and as your business grows, invest in more specialized tools that can handle increased complexity and provide greater value. Ultimately, the best CRM is the one you use.

Choosing the Right Tools

Selecting the right tools for your business involves considering your specific needs, budget, and the scale of your operations. Here are some tips to guide your choice:

- **Evaluate your needs**: Assess the size of your audience, the frequency of your engagements, and the complexity of your interactions. Choose tools that match your current requirements but can scale as you grow.
- **Consider integration capabilities**: Ensure that the CRM system you choose can integrate seamlessly with other tools you use, such as email marketing software, social media platforms, and accounting systems.
- **User-friendliness**: Opt for CRMs that are intuitive and easy to navigate. The less time you spend learning to use the tool, the more time you can spend engaging with your audience and growing your business.
- **Support and resources**: This is especially important for technology that plays a critical role in your business. Choose providers that offer reliable customer support and have a strong user community or resource base.

By equipping yourself with the right business tools, you can focus more on delivering great content and less on the administrative burdens that come with running a speaking business. These tools not only aid in maintaining professionalism but also ensure that you can keep up with the demands as your business expands.

Starting Small But Smart

Starting a speaking business while managing other personal and professional responsibilities is challenging, but it can be done with strategic planning and a lot of dedication. Here's how I navigated this dual commitment early in my career:

Maximizing Time

- **Weekend Speaking Engagements**: I leveraged my vacation days to free up Thursdays, Fridays, and Mondays, allowing me to travel for speaking engagements over the weekend.
- **Efficient Travel**: Flights were scheduled for Thursday nights post-work, maximizing the use of time for travel, speaking on Friday and Saturday, and returning home on Sundays.
- **Quick Turnaround**: This schedule meant I was back at my desk by Monday morning, ready for another work week.

The Reality of the Hustle

- **Physical and Mental Demands**: Yes, the schedule was grueling. It required significant personal sacrifice and stamina.

- **Family Impact**: It wasn't just me making sacrifices; my family, particularly my wife, felt the strain of my absence during these days.

Building a Foundation

- **Gradual Transition**: I maintained this pace for two years, which laid a solid foundation for my speaking business. This period allowed me to build my reputation, expand my network, and refine my presentations.
- **Transition to Full-time**: The effort paid off as it eventually led to enough bookings and financial stability to transition into full-time speaking and consulting.

Tips for Aspiring Speakers

- **Start Small**: Begin with local or less demanding speaking engagements to manage travel and time effectively.
- **Plan Meticulously**: Use a calendar to plan your engagements around your other priorities to reduce conflicts.
- **Set Measurable Goals**: Have a timeline for when you want to increase your efforts to directly contact event planners and decision makers, which will help you measure your progress and stay motivated.

- **Engage Support**: Communicate with your support system (i.e. family, friends, fans, etc.) about your goals and the demands of your schedule. Their support is crucial.

> **Phipps Tip:** The journey can be as challenging as it is rewarding. While it's important to push for growth, also ensure you're not sacrificing too much personal well-being. Balance is key, even when ambition runs high.

By starting small and smart, you can build a speaking business without immediately giving up the security of a full-time job. This approach minimizes risk and provides a practical pathway to achieving your dreams in professional speaking.

Volunteering to speak can be a powerful tool for new speakers to gain experience, build their portfolio, and make essential industry connections. However, it's important to approach these opportunities strategically to ensure they're beneficial for your career growth.

The Value of Strategic Volunteering

- **Case Example**: Early in my career, I agreed to speak at a hospital conference without a speaker's fee. In exchange, I negotiated several key benefits:
    - **Professional Video Recording**: This provided me with high-quality footage of my presentation, which I could use for marketing and promotional purposes.
    - **Professional Photos**: Similarly, professional photographs from the event enhanced my marketing materials and online presence.
    - **Access to Conference Sessions**: Attending other sessions allowed me to learn, network, and stay informed about industry trends.
    - **Introduction to Key Decision-Makers**: Being introduced to important figures at the conference helped me expand my professional network, leading to more opportunities.

Leveraging Free or Low-Paying Engagements

- **Tangible Returns**: Look for tangible returns when agreeing to speak for free or when significantly lowering your fee. These can include promotional materials, networking opportunities, data collection (i.e., email

addresses for your newsletter, contact names, and attendee registrations), or endorsements.
- **Targeted Exposure**: Choose events that align closely with your niche or where your target audience will be present. This maximizes the relevance and impact of your exposure.

> **Phipps Tip**: Never speak for "free" in the absolute sense. Ensure that you're compensated in ways that advance your career, such as exposure, media content, testimonials, or direct introductions to potential clients.

Building from Volunteer Speaking Engagements

- **Follow-Up**: After a volunteer speaking engagement, follow up with contacts made during the event. Express gratitude, provide additional value, and keep the lines of communication open.
- **Use Materials**: Utilize the videos and photos obtained to enhance your website, social media, and other marketing channels. These materials can significantly improve your credibility and attract paying clients.

- **Measure ROI**: Keep track of the return on investment from these engagements, including any subsequent paid opportunities that arise as a direct result. This will help you assess whether your strategy for volunteering is effective.

By adopting a strategic approach to volunteer speaking engagements, you can transform what might seem like a freebie into a valuable stepping stone in your speaking career.

When launching your speaking business, it's important to understand the initial costs and investments required to establish a professional presence. Here's a practical checklist to help you budget effectively and prioritize your spending:

Speaker Business Startup Budget List

Legal Classifications

Business Setup Item	Estimated Cost	Notes
LLC Formation	$200–$500	Enhances credibility and

		provides legal protection. Check your state for exact filing fees
Sole Proprietorship	$0–$100	Enhances credibility and provides legal protection. Check your state for exact filing fees.
Business Registration/ Name Reservation	$50–$150	Some states require this even for sole proprietors
EIN (Employer Identification Number)	Free	Apply through the IRS website. Needed for business banking and taxes.

Branding & Marketing

Item	Estimated Cost	Notes
Professional Website	$500–$1,500	Include bio, speaking topics, video, testimonials, and contact form.
Domain & Hosting	$50–$150/year	Make sure to get a professional domain (e.g., yourname.com).
Professional Headshots	$300–$800	Use for website, speaker one-sheet, and social media.
Business Cards	$50–$100	Still useful at networking events and conferences.

		Include a QR code on your site.
Speaker One-Sheet (Design)	$100–$300	A concise marketing document summarizing your expertise and offers

Operations & Tools

Item	Estimated Cost	Notes
CRM System	$20–$100/month	Use to manage leads, track proposals, and nurture contacts.

Accounting Software	$20–$40/month	Options: QuickBooks, Wave, or FreshBooks. Great for invoices and tax prep.
Email Marketing Platform	$0–$50/month	Use Mailchimp, ConvertKit, etc. for lead nurturing and newsletters.
Scheduling Tool	$10–$25/month	Tools like Calendly make it easy to book calls or consultations.

Content & Development

Item	Estimated Cost	Notes

Speaker Demo Video	$0–$1,500	Start with volunteer footage; upgrade as you grow.
Graphic Design Tools	$10–$20/month	Canva Pro or Adobe Express for presentations and visuals.
Virtual Presentation Equipment	$200–$600	Basic setup: ring light, webcam, quality mic, and backdrop.
Professional Development	$100–$1,0000	Speaking courses, coaching, or NSA membership ($500+/year).

$mart Cost-$aving Tips

- **Barter or trade services** (e.g., speak for a videographer's event in exchange for footage).

- **Start with low-cost or DIY options** (e.g., Wix or Squarespace website, Canva speaker sheet).

- **Apply for microgrants** to offset early-stage business costs.

- **Bundle services**—some platforms offer CRM, email marketing, and landing pages in one.

My Advice: Start simple. You don't need the most expensive tools or services at the beginning. Prioritize the essentials that present you professionally and upgrade as your revenue increases.

Strategic Investment Tips

- **Focus on Essentials**: Initially, invest in necessities that directly contribute to acquiring clients and delivering your services.
- **Reinvest Profits**: As you start earning, reinvest a portion of your profits to enhance your business tools and marketing efforts.

> **Phipps Tip**: While it's tempting to buy the best of everything at the start, financial prudence will serve you better. Begin with what is necessary for operation and presentation, then gradually upgrade as your business grows and demands more sophisticated tools and services.

This checklist not only helps in budgeting wisely but also ensures that you're set up for success with a solid foundation without overspending.

Types of Speaking Engagements

Understanding the different types of speaking engagements can help you strategically position yourself in the market and maximize your revenue. Here's a breakdown of the main types of speaking opportunities and what they entail:

Keynote Speaking

- **Duration**: Typically 45-90 minutes
- **Setting**: Delivered on the main stage, often as the highlight of the event

- **Compensation**: Generally, the highest-paying speaking opportunity
- **Focus**: Keynote speeches are designed to inspire and motivate, setting the tone for the event with big ideas and powerful narratives

Breakout Sessions

- **Duration**: Usually 60-90 minutes
- **Interactivity**: More interactive than keynotes and allowing for more audience engagement and discussion
- **Content**: Focused on specific topics, providing deeper insights or practical applications
- **Context**: These sessions are often part of larger conferences, offering attendees a choice of specialized topics

Workshop Facilitation

- **Length**: Can be half-day or full-day sessions
- **Interactivity**: Highly interactive, involving participant activities and practical exercises
- **Depth**: Workshops provide a deep dive into specific skills or knowledge areas
- **Materials**: Often includes workbooks, handouts, or other educational materials to enhance learning

Virtual Speaking

- **Format**: Includes online presentations, webinars, virtual conferences, and remote workshops
- **Flexibility**: Virtual speaking allows you to reach a global audience without travel expenses
- **Technology**: Requires proficiency with digital tools and platforms to deliver engaging and interactive sessions

---

Phipps Tip: Start gaining experience with various types of engagements. Even if the fees are modest initially, focus on delivering exceptional value. This will build your reputation and can lead to more lucrative opportunities.

Revenue Streams

While speaking fees are significant, they shouldn't be your only source of income. Diversifying your revenue streams can provide financial stability and leverage your expertise more broadly.

Multiple Revenue Streams for Speakers:

- **Publications**: Offering books and articles for content reinforcement
- **Online Courses**: Developing and selling content in a virtual format
- **Consulting**: Leveraging expertise to existing companies and organizations
- **Merchandising**: Creating branded tools to complement strategies and techniques
- **Sponsorships**: Partnering to collaborate a shared training vision
- **Keynotes:** Delivering mainstage presentations
- **Workshops:** Facilitating interactive classes and seminars
- **Coaching:** Customizing one-on-one development strategies
- **Licensures:** Allocating content for limited access

Phipps Tip: Consider your speaking engagements as a platform for multiple revenue opportunities. By diversifying your income sources, you not only increase your earning potential but also create a more resilient business model.

By understanding these different types of speaking engagements and considering multiple revenue streams, you can build a robust speaking career that maximizes both impact and income.

Revenue Streams: Multiple Ways to Monetize Your Expertise

Successful speakers don't just rely on speaking fees; they diversify their income to maximize earnings and ensure financial stability. Here's how you can do the same by tapping into various revenue streams:

1. Direct Speaking Income

- **Keynote Speaking**: Fees range from waived fees to hundreds of thousands for main stage presentations, depending on the event and your profile.
- **Breakout Sessions**: Smaller, more focused sessions can fetch between a few hundred to a few thousand.
- **Panel Moderation**: Can be paid per speaker or one fee divided amongst the panelists.
- **Example**: After securing a $5,000 keynote, I negotiated two additional breakout sessions for

a total of $8,500, leveraging a single trip for maximum revenue.

2. Products and Materials

- **Books**: Selling books at events can significantly boost income. For instance, selling a book for $25 can add up if 20% of a 200-person audience buys one.
- **Online Courses**: Offer courses ranging from several hundred for an introductory course up to several thousands for premium content.
- **Example**: Selling an online course at an event can quickly add thousands to your income, as seen when 15 attendees signed up, netting $7,455 in extra revenue.

3. Back-of-Room Sales Strategy

- **Triple Play**: Offer a combination of low, mid, and high-priced items to cater to different buyer thresholds at events.
- **Example**: Selling books, courses, and coaching packages can yield nearly $5,000 from a 100-person audience.

4. Recurring Revenue Models

- **Membership Programs**: Monthly fees from memberships can provide a steady income stream.

- **Coaching Programs**: High-value coaching services can range from a few hundred to thousands of dollars per month.
- **Training Licensing**: Licensing your content to other trainers or corporations can generate substantial annual revenue.
- **Recurring Programs:** quarterly or biannual follow-ups or continuations

5. Strategic Partnerships

- **Corporate Sponsorships**: Partnering with brands can lead to lucrative deals, such as sponsored talks or brand ambassador roles.
- **Example**: A partnership with a software company brought in $60,000 from 12 events in a year.

6. Digital Products

- **Assessment Tools and Training Materials**: Create digital products that can be sold repeatedly, generating passive income.
- **Example**: Spending time developing a comprehensive training program can pay off in continuous passive revenue.

Revenue Stacking Strategy

- **Example**: A single speaking engagement can potentially generate several thousand dollars by combining fees from keynote speaking, book sales, online course enrollments, emailed or printed materials, coaching, and corporate packages.

Implementation Tips:

- **Start with One Stream**: Master one revenue stream before adding others
- **Pre-Create Products**: Have your products ready before you need them, ensuring you can seize every sales opportunity
- **Automate Sales**: Develop systems to handle sales processes, allowing you to focus on delivering value
- **Continuous Value Creation**: Always look for new ways to offer value, ensuring your offerings remain relevant and sought after

---

Phipps Tip: Aim to at least achieve 50% of your speaking fee and materials through additional revenue streams at every engagement.

By diversifying your income sources and strategically stacking your revenue streams, you can turn each speaking engagement into a significant business opportunity, ensuring that you're not just a speaker but a savvy entrepreneur in the speaking industry.

Action Steps Checklist: Getting Your Speaking Business Started

Starting a speaking business involves several structured steps. Following this comprehensive checklist will ensure you set up your business effectively and professionally.

1. Business Foundation Setup

  A. **Choose your business structure**: LLC, Sole Proprietorship, etc.
  B. **Apply for an EIN**: Essential for tax purposes and to establish your business legally
  C. **Open a business bank account**: Keeps your personal and business finances separate
  D. **Set up a business email and phone number**: Provides others with contact information
  E. **Purchase basic accounting software**: Helps manage finances and taxes
  F. **Set up a CRM system**: Crucial for managing contact relationships and bookings
  G. **Get business insurance**: Protects against liabilities and unforeseen circumstances

2. Brand Development

A. **Define your target audience:** Understand who will benefit most from your speaking.
B. **Clarify your core message:** Define your industry skills and expertise.
C. **Create an elevator pitch:** Develop a concise description of what you do and how it matters.
D. **Have Professional headshots:** Use high-quality head and torso photographs.
E. **Design your logo, choose brand colors and fonts, design business cards and presentation templates:** Remain consistent across all materials to strengthen your brand identity.

3. Online Presence

A. **Purchase a domain name and build a basic website:** Your digital storefront.
B. **Set up professional social media accounts and LinkedIn profile:** Essential for networking and promotion.
C. **Start an email list and create a speaker one-sheet:** Tools to communicate directly with your audience and promote your services concisely.

4. Content Development

A. **Write three signature stories and develop a core presentation**: Foundations of your speaking content.
B. **Create presentation slides and handouts/worksheets**: Enhances audience engagement.
C. **Record a demo video and write a speaker bio in various lengths**: Critical for marketing and booking speaking engagements.

5. Revenue Stream Setup

A. **Set speaking fee structure and create tiered pricing packages**: Allows flexibility and maximizes revenue potential.
B. **Develop at least one additional product, such as a book or course**: Diversifies income sources.
C. **Set up payment processing and create a speaker agreement template**: Streamlines financial transactions and formalizes engagements.

6. Marketing Foundation

A. **Join professional speaking organizations**: Associate with other speakers.

B. **Acquire a lead generation system:** Expands your network and sources potential engagements.
   C. **Set up a speaking calendar and develop proposal and follow-up email templates:** Organize your outreach and follow-up processes.
   D. **Set up a testimonial collection system:** Builds credibility through client feedback.

7. Business Operations

   A. **Create filing and expense tracking systems:** Keeps your business organized and accountable.
   B. **Have the following tracking systems:**
      1) Travel checklist and
      2) Pre-event questionnaire
      3) Mileage tracking system

8. First 90 Days Goals

   A. **Book your first speaking engagement (paid or unpaid):** Puts your skills to the test.
   B. **Collect three testimonials and create video footage of your speaking:** Builds credibility and marketing materials.
   C. **Connect with at least five potential clients:** Establish your pipeline.
   D. **Join two professional organizations:** Affiliate yourself with industry leaders.

E. **Attend an industry event**: Expands your network and exposure.
F. **Create one lead magnet**: Attracts subscribers and potential leads.

Phipps Tips:

- **Don't wait for perfection**: Start with the essentials and improve as you go.
- **Complete one section at a time and regularly review and update your checklist**: Ensures continuous improvement.
- **Track progress and celebrate small wins**: Keeps you motivated and focused on growth.

Remember, you're not just becoming a speaker; you're building a business. Treat it with the seriousness it deserves from day one, and you'll be well on your way to establishing a successful speaking career. Next, we'll explore how to develop your speaking foundation and create content that resonates with audiences, helping you to stand out in this competitive field.

Chapter 2: Your Speaking Foundation

Developing Your Core Message

Successful speakers know that a clear, resonant message is critical. It's not about covering all bases; it's about targeting your strengths and passions to meet specific needs. Here's how to refine your core message into something both compelling and marketable.

Finding Your Sweet Spot

To discover the niche where you'll thrive, consider three critical factors:

1. **What do you know deeply?** Your expertise should come from a profound understanding of the subject.
2. **Where will people invest?** Your knowledge must solve an existing problem.
3. **What is your passion?** Genuine enthusiasm for your topic will not only enhance your presentations but also sustain your motivation.

Real Example: In the early days, I offered general communication skills training—broad and somewhat bland. Then, I identified a niche: IT professionals who struggled to convey complex technical concepts to non-technical audiences. This revelation was pivotal in helping me develop a niche for providing strategies to make those technical presentations easier to understand.

> **Phipps Tip:** Emulate success but don't copy it. Instead of trying to be the next Tony Robbins Brené Brown, or Les Brown focus on being the best version of yourself, addressing specific issues for specific audiences.

Niching Down

The specificity can significantly enhance your appeal and business prospects. Here's how to focus your offerings:

General vs. Specific:

- Instead of saying *"I help people communicate better,"* specify *"I assist technical professionals in communicating complex ideas to non-technical stakeholders."*
- Rather than saying *"I'm a leadership speaker,"* narrow it down to *"I aid first-time managers in healthcare to develop leadership skills that enhance patient care."*

Real Example: A graduate from my 3-Day Masterclass, Pro Speaker's Kit (PSK), struggled to gain traction until she focused her message. Moving from a general "women's empowerment" theme to becoming "the expert who assists female entrepreneurs in confidently pricing their services," she saw her bookings triple within six months.

The TRUE Technique

Craft a message that resonates and differentiates you using the TRUE formula:

- **T - Target:** Identify who specifically needs your message. What is the industry/organization/community you are serving?
- **R - Rationale:** Understand why your audience needs your message now. What current challenges or opportunities make your offering relevant?
- **U - Uniqueness:** Clarify what makes your approach distinct. Why should an event planner or attendee choose you over others?
- **E - Expertise:** Showcase your credentials and experiences that qualify you to speak on the topic. What have you accomplished that validates you as an expert?

Vincentism: Just because you like to order food doesn't make you a customer service expert.

By deeply understanding and applying these elements, you can craft a core message that not only defines your brand but also makes you highly sought after in the speaking world. Each element of the TRUE technique helps you build a compelling narrative around your speaking career, ensuring that you are not just heard but also remembered and valued.

The TRUE Technique - In Action

T - Target

Weak Example: *"I speak to businesses about leadership."*
Strong Example: *"I help mid-level managers in manufacturing companies develop leadership skills to reduce turnover and improve production efficiency."*

Real-World Applications:

1. **Healthcare Speaker**

   Target: *"First-year nursing managers in hospitals with 200+ beds"*

   Why It Works: This target is highly specific, addressing a distinct group within the healthcare industry by pinpointing their role, experience level, and the scale of their organization. This specificity ensures the content is directly relevant and highly applicable, increasing the value and impact of the message.

2. **Sales Speaker**

   Target: *"B2B software sales teams transitioning from field sales to virtual selling"*

   Why It Works: By naming the industry, role, and specific transition challenge, the speaker aligns their message with the immediate needs of their audience. This helps in addressing pertinent issues that are top of mind for the audience, making the sessions highly practical and urgently relevant.

3. **DEI Speaker**

   Target: *"HR directors in Fortune 1000 companies implementing diversity initiatives in hybrid workplaces"*

   Why It Works: This targeting is effective because it not only specifies the role and company size but also focuses on a current challenge that is impacting a large segment of the corporate world. It ensures that the content delivered is tailored to the unique complexities of managing diversity in modern, evolving workplace environments.

Story Time

In an example from my own experience, I tailored a presentation for a trucking industry conference by adapting all examples to reflect the day-to-day realities of that specific industry. Instead of generic business scenarios, I referred to real trucking situations, like interactions with dispatchers. This approach was met with significant appreciation from the organizer, who noted it was the first time a speaker had truly spoken "their language." This not only enhanced engagement but also boosted the practical value of the information provided.

Takeaway

Effective targeting in speaking involves more than understanding your audience—it requires a deep dive into their specific challenges, work environment, and industry trends. This approach ensures that your speeches are not just heard but are impactful, driving change and fostering a strong connection with your audience. Always aim to tailor your message so finely that each member feels like you're speaking directly to them, addressing their unique circumstances and needs.

R - Rationale

<u>Weak Example:</u> *"Leadership is important."* **<u>Strong Example</u>:** *"With 40% of manufacturing leaders retiring in the next five years, developing new leaders is critical for maintaining production standards and preventing costly mistakes."*

Real-World Applications:

1. **Technology Sector**

   Rationale: *"As AI transforms software development, technical teams need new communication skills to collaborate with AI tools and non-technical stakeholders."*

   Why It Works: This rationale is effective because it taps into the prevailing trend of AI integration into software development. It emphasizes the necessity for enhanced communication skills, linking the development of these skills directly to the audience's ability to stay relevant and effective in their rapidly changing field.

2. **Financial Services**

   Rationale: *"With new SEC regulations taking effect next quarter, financial advisors need updated compliance communication strategies."*

   Why It Works: This argument is strong because it addresses an immediate regulatory change, making the need for updated communication strategies urgent and relevant. It connects the speaker's message directly to the audience's need to adapt quickly to remain compliant and effective.

3. **Education**

    Rationale: *"Post-pandemic learning gaps require new teaching approaches to help students catch up while preventing educator burnout."*

    Why It Works: This rationale speaks directly to a significant ongoing issue in the education sector. It highlights the dual need to address learning gaps and protect instructors' well-being, making the speaker's proposed solutions both critical and timely.

Real Life Example

When I pitch to IT companies, I highlight a common inefficiency: technical teams spend approximately 40% of their time explaining projects to non-technical stakeholders. I then pose a question about the cost of this inefficiency in terms of time and resources. This approach not only underscores the financial impact of the problem but also positions my speaking services as a cost-effective solution, emphasizing the return on investment that my expertise can offer.

Why It Works: By quantifying the impact of the problem and linking it directly to a financial metric, the rationale makes the need for my services immediate and quantifiable. This strategy effectively turns the cost of my speaking fee into a wise investment for potential clients, showcasing the tangible benefits of improving communication within their teams.

Takeaway

A well-crafted rationale is essential for making your speaking topic resonate with your audience. It should not only identify a problem but also connect your message to the audience's immediate needs and priorities. By demonstrating how your insights can solve current challenges or capitalize on emerging opportunities, you provide compelling reasons for organizations to invest in your speaking services.

U - Uniqueness

Weak Example: *"I'm passionate about leadership."*
Strong Example: *"I developed my leadership approach while managing emergency response teams in Antarctica, where every decision could be life-or-death."*

Real-World Applications:

1. **Sales Training**

    Traditional Approach: *"I teach sales techniques."*

Unique Approach: *"I teach sales psychology based on my research with professional poker players and hostage negotiators."*

Why It Works: This approach captivates interest by linking sales strategies to high-stakes poker and negotiation scenarios, which include increased awareness of non-verbal communication and vocal patterns to provide a fresh and intriguing perspective that promises innovative insights and tactics far beyond traditional sales methods.

2. **Change Management**

    Traditional Approach: *"I help companies manage change."*

    Unique Approach: *"I apply NASA's mission control protocols to help companies navigate major transitions."*

    Why It Works: By associating change management strategies with NASA's proven protocols, this approach not only elevates the credibility of the methods but also intrigues audiences with its application of high-level, critical success strategies to business environments.

3. **Team Building**

    Traditional Approach: "I help teams work better together."

    Customized Approach: "I use my experience as a professional orchestra conductor to teach teams about harmony and coordination."

    Why It Works: This unique angle draws a vivid analogy between orchestrating music and orchestrating team dynamics, offering a novel perspective that makes the concept of team synergy both understandable and memorable.

Real Life Example

One of the most powerful transformations I've witnessed came from a speaker in my Pro Speakers Kit (PSK) masterclass. She started her speaking career with a focus on communication, but her bookings were stagnant. Despite having strong content, she sounded like every other communication speaker out there—until she tapped into her *true edge*.

She was a former **air traffic controller**, someone used to making split-second decisions under immense pressure. When she began integrating that experience into her keynotes—talking about communication when lives are on the line, when clarity cuts through chaos—everything changed. Suddenly, her talks weren't just about "better communication"—they were about **mission-critical clarity**. Bookings skyrocketed.

The same was true for another PSK member, **Becky**. She wanted to break into **corporate America** with a message around empowerment and personal safety, but her background wasn't "corporate." She came from a career in **munitions and self-defense training**. At first, she struggled. "What can I teach people who sit at a desk?" she asked.

During Day 2 of Pro Speakers Kit (PSK) we practiced customization techniques. That's when her question was reframed to the following: "*What do people in corporate America need that I uniquely understand?*" That's when it clicked.

Becky built a signature program showing professionals how to use **everyday office items**—like a **credit card, business card, or even a stapler**—as tools of **personal safety and empowerment**. She wasn't teaching people how to fight; she was teaching them how to feel **confident, aware,** and **prepared** in any setting—whether walking to their car at night, heading to the gym, or traveling for work. She turned a background that once felt like a mismatch into a **marketable, unforgettable niche**.

Why It Works: Her **specialized experience** delivered a **distinct and practical message**. She offered **relevant, everyday applications** her audience hadn't seen before. It gave her a unique **category an area of expertise** that very few others were offering.

Takeaway: Your Background Is Your Brand

Your uniqueness isn't an aside—it's your advantage. In an industry where audiences are flooded with generic content, what makes you **different** is what makes you **valuable**.

Whether your edge is:

- An **unusual career path**

- An **unexpected life experience**

- Or a **hyper-specific skillset**…

…**it belongs at the center of your message**. When you **own** your story and **weave it strategically** into your speaking platform, you move from being a speaker to being a solution—and that's what event planners are really booking.

> **Reminder**: You don't have to be like everyone else to succeed—you just have to be *fully and strategically* yourself.

E – Expertise

<u>Weak Example:</u> "I'm really good at what I do." **Strong** <u>Strong Example:</u> "I've reduced turnover by 40% in 50 manufacturing teams using a leadership model backed by my 15 years of experience and research from an MIT study."

Expertise Stack Examples

1. **Corporate Speaker**
    - **Education**: MBA, Six Sigma Black Belt
    - **Experience**: 19 years in Fortune 500 companies
    - **Results**: Led to 97 successful mergers
    - **Recognition**: Featured in Forbes
    - **Research**: Published industry studies
2. **Healthcare Speaker**
    - **Clinical Experience**: 16 years as a Registered Nurse
    - **Leadership**: Former Hospital Chief of Staff
    - **Academic**: PhD in Healthcare Administration
    - **Research**: Published in medical journals
    - **Results**: Developed a protocol used in over 100 hospitals
3. **Technology Speaker**
    - **Technical**: Former Software Architect
    - **Business**: Built and sold two tech startups

- **Teaching**: Adjunct Professor at Stanford
- **Writing**: Author of three technical books
- **Media**: Regular CNBC contributor

Phipps Tips for Building Expertise

Start Where You Are

- **Document Your Results**: Keep a detailed record of your achievements and the impact of your work.
- **Gather Testimonials**: Collect feedback from every engagement to build validation for prospective clients.
- **Write Articles:** Share your knowledge and insights regularly to establish thought leadership.
- **Blog Posts**: Identify current industry trends to offer insights and solutions.
- **Start and/or be a guest on Podcasts:** Use this to build a digital platform to highlight your expertise.
- **Create Case Studies**: Showcase specific examples of how your work has produced positive outcomes.

Strategic Enhancement

- **Pursue Relevant Certifications**: Update your qualifications to stay relevant in your field.
- **Join Industry Boards**: Enhance your profile by getting involved in the decision-making within your industry.
- **Conduct Original Research**: Engage in research to contribute new knowledge or expand on existing studies.
- **Collaborate with Recognized Experts**: Work with established names to gain credibility and expand your network.

Phipps Tip: You don't need to have every type of expertise, but you need enough credibility to make hiring you a 'safe' and beneficial decision for every event planner.

Integrating the TRUE Technique

The effectiveness of the TRUE technique lies in its integrated approach:

- **Target** - align your message with the demographic that needs it most.
- **Rationale** - identify the pending or existing problem that your message addresses.
- **Uniqueness** - speak with authenticity about why you feel this message has significance.
- **Expertise** - incorporate your training and education to position yourself as an expert.

Action Exercise:

1. **Define Your Target**: How can you be ruthlessly specific?
2. **List Your Rationale**: Why is your message critical right now?
3. **Identify Your Uniqueness**: What unique angle or approach do you offer?
4. **Outline Your Expertise**: What are your topic qualifications, experiences, and achievements?

Vincentism: No one cares if you won 2nd place in the spelling-bee in the 5th grade.

Share this refined concept with at least five people within your target market. Their feedback will provide valuable insights into whether your presentation resonates and addresses the needs and interests of potential clients effectively. This exercise not only sharpens your message but also tests its market relevance, ensuring you're on track to engage and impact your audience profoundly.

Building Your Signature Stories: Glory Stories

Creating Glory Stories is essential for any speaker aiming to connect deeply with their audience. These stories not only make your presentations more engaging but also help establish your authority and relatability. Here's how to craft compelling signature Glory Stories:

1. The Credential Story

Strong Example: *"The Million-Dollar Mistake"*

Context: *"As a young IT manager, I was tasked with presenting to the board during a critical meeting."*

Conflict: *"I had to explain why our system crashed during the busiest season of the year."*

Choice: *"I chose to use dense technical jargon, hoping to sound more knowledgeable and in control."*

Consequence: *"The board didn't grasp the urgency or implications, resulting in a $1 million loss in sales."*

Connection: *"This disastrous outcome led me to develop a straightforward communication framework that I now teach."*

Why It Works: This story is powerful because it features a specific incident with high stakes and a clear transformation. The speaker's personal mistake and the tangible consequences highlight the need for the expertise they now offer.

Phipps Tip: Your Glory Story should illustrate a pivotal moment that compelled you to become an expert in your field. It should underline your qualifications and set the stage for why listeners should trust your insights. Glory stories don't always have you as the hero. It's ok to acknowledge where you made a mistake and how you fixed it (like in the above example).

2. The Connection Story

Strong Example: *"The Airport Moment"*

Situation: *"I was rushing through Atlanta's airport, focused on my phone, when I collided with an elderly man."*

Impact: *"As I helped him up, he told me, 'Son, you're so busy going somewhere, you're missing being somewhere.'"*

Realization: *"His words struck me profoundly. Despite teaching leadership, I wasn't practicing what I preached."*

Transformation: *"This encounter forced me to reevaluate my priorities and truly embody the leadership principles I teach."*

Why It Works: This story resonates because it's relatable and includes a memorable, transformative moment. It conveys a personal realization that enhances the speaker's authenticity and connects emotionally with the audience.

Vincentism: We think we're good at it until we have to use it! How are you going to be a dentist and have raggedy teeth?! How are you going to be a personal trainer and walk up to me, eating a Twinkie, telling me that you didn't eat anything today?

3. The Change Story

Structure Example: *"The Three-Month Turnaround"*

Before: *"Our team was suffering from a 40% turnover rate."*

Trigger: *"An eye-opening exit interview revealed the lack of effective communication."*

Process: *"We decided to implement a new, inclusive communication strategy."*

Challenge: *"Despite initial resistance from senior management, we persisted."*

Breakthrough: *"Junior staff members began to embrace and lead the change."*

After: *"The turnover rate dropped to 5% within three months."*

Lesson: *"This experience taught us that leadership can, and should, come from every level within an organization."*

Why It Works: This story demonstrates a clear before-and-after scenario that showcases the speaker's ability to drive significant change. It highlights their expertise in solving complex problems and making impactful decisions.

> **Phipps Tip:** Develop multiple versions of each story to fit different contexts and time constraints. This flexibility allows you to dynamically adjust your storytelling to match the audience and setting.

30-second version: A quick synopsis that captures the essence of the story.

2-minute version: A more detailed version that outlines key moments and insights.

5-minute version: An in-depth narrative that fully explores the context, conflict, and resolution.

Crafting signature Glory Stories requires thoughtful reflection on your experiences, the lessons you've learned, and how they relate to your message. Each story should be structured to not only entertain but also to enlighten, providing valuable insights that underscore your key speaking points. By integrating these stories into your presentations, you enhance your connection with the audience, making your message both memorable and impactful.

Content Architecture for Engaging Presentations

Creating a compelling structure for your presentations is crucial for keeping the audience engaged and delivering your message effectively. Here are detailed frameworks for constructing your opening, core content, and closing sections:

1. Opening Frameworks

The "PUNCH" Opening:

This framework is designed to grab the audience's attention right from the start and set up the context for your presentation.

Problem: Start by clearly stating the challenge or issue at hand.

Urgency: Highlight why this issue is critical and needs to be addressed now.

Need: Explain what's at stake if the problem is unresolved.

Credibility: Establish why you are the right person to address this issue.

Hope: End your opening by outlining what is possible and what the audience can look forward to learning.

Example PUNCH Opening: *"Currently, 67% of IT projects fail due to communication gaps. As digital transformation picks up speed, this problem is worsening. Each failed project can cost companies an average of $1.1M. Over the past decade, I've helped 97 companies bridge this gap effectively. Today, I'll share three proven strategies that can help reduce these failures by up to 79%."*

2. Core Content Structures

The "PAR" Framework:

This framework helps you deliver your core content in a structured and impactful way.

Point: Assert the main idea or statement of your segment.

Action: Describe actionable steps the audience can take based on the point you've made.

Result: Illustrate the potential or actual outcomes that follow from taking these actions.

Example PAR Block: Technical jargon often creates barriers to understanding and can isolate non-technical stakeholders. A simple solution is to use the '5th Grade Test'—explain technical concepts as you would to a typical 5th grader. This approach helped one of our teams cut their meeting times in half, as everyone understood the points being made quickly.

3. Closing Frameworks

The "CLOSE" Method:

This method ensures that your closing is as powerful as your opening and reinforces your key messages.

Circle: Refer back to the opening to bring the presentation full circle.

Lead: Provide clear next steps or actions for the audience to take.

Overcome: Anticipate and address potential objections or hesitations.

Story: Share a final, inspiring story that encapsulates your message.

Engage: End with a strong call to action, encouraging the audience to take specific steps.

Example CLOSE: "Remember the $1.1M project failure rate I mentioned at the start? Here are the first three steps you can take to start closing the gap in your organization. You might think, 'We don't have time for this.' However, consider the alternative costs of inaction. Let me tell you about a team that decided to implement these strategies despite their initial hesitations. They saw a 70% decrease in project delays within six months. Who's ready to transform their team and start seeing similar results?"

Using these frameworks, you can structure your presentation to maximize clarity, engagement, and impact. Each part serves to guide your audience through your message systematically and persuasively, ensuring that they leave with a clear understanding of your key points and are motivated to take action.

Building Credibility: A Comprehensive Guide

Creating and presenting a compelling credibility profile is crucial for establishing trust and authority in your field. Here's how to effectively build and showcase your credibility across different layers:

1. Foundation Layer

Academic Credentials:

- Degrees in relevant fields
- Certifications that enhance your expertise
- Specialized training that sets you apart
- Continuing education to stay current in your industry

Experience Metrics:

- Years of experience in your industry
- Number of clients served or consulted
- Projects completed successfully
- Total presentations or workshops given

Professional Development:

- Industry-specific certifications

- Technical qualifications that add depth to your expertise
- Leadership roles within organizations
- Active participation in committees or professional groups

2. Proof Layer

Client Results Database:

- Detailed examples of client success, like a 41% productivity increase at Company A, $2.2M savings implemented at Company B, or a 59% reduction in team turnover at Company C.

Case Study Format:

- Outline challenges faced by clients.
- Describe solutions you implemented.
- Highlight results achieved.
- Include client testimonials and supporting data to verify claims.

Media Presence:

- Podcast appearances discussing industry topics
- Quotes in articles or feature stories
- Interview segments on media: television, radio, publications, etc.
- Participation in relevant social media outlets

3. Authority Layer

Industry Recognition:

- Awards or accolades received

- Patents held
- Research published in respected journals or publications (Wikipedia doesn't count)
- Rankings within industry metrics or evaluations

Board Positions:

- Roles in professional associations
- Membership on industry committees
- Advisory positions on boards
- Leadership within nonprofit organizations

Notable Clients:

- Work with Fortune 500 companies, government agencies, major institutions, or recognized industry leaders.
- Request permission from clients to share their success stories with future audiences.

4. Social Proof Layer

Digital Presence:

- Website traffic statistics
- Size of your email subscriber list
- Social media following and interaction
- Video view counts on platforms like YouTube

Engagement Metrics:

- Comments and shares on social media posts
- Attendance at workshops or seminars
- Rates of program completion

- Repeat booking rates for speaking engagements

Community Building:

- Management of online groups related to your field
- Active participation in forums
- Influence and thought leadership within industry discussions

---

Phipps Tip: Create a Credibility Package

Assemble an electronic document that includes:

- 2 Introductions/Biographies: The first 50 words or less the other should be 150 words or less
- A compilation of clients achieved objectives
- A list of clients and services delivered
- Testimonials in video, written and quantifiable formats
- Documentation/Hyperlinks of media appearances
- A calendar of past, pending and future speaking engagements

Action Steps for Building Credibility:

- **Audit Current Credibility Assets**:

    Align your expertise with your core message to show validity.

- **Identify Gaps in Each Layer**:

    Determine what areas are lacking and need enhancement.

- **Create a 90-Day Plan to Fill Gaps**:

    Set goals to acquire new credentials, gain more client testimonials, increase media presence, etc.

- **Document All Results**:

    Update your professional portfolio/resume with new clients, developments, services, products, and endeavors.

- **Update Materials Quarterly**:

    Regularly refresh your credibility package and online profiles to reflect new achievements.

- **Collect Testimonials Consistently**:

    Actively seek feedback in the form of surveys and endorsements from clients and colleagues.

- **Track All Media Mentions**:

    Keep a record of all times you are mentioned in the media for use in your credibility documents.

Remember: Credibility isn't just about possessing qualifications and results; it's about effectively presenting them. Package and showcase your credibility in a way that makes hiring you a no-brainer for any event planner or client. This strategic presentation ensures that your expertise is recognized and valued, paving the way for new opportunities and continued success.

Action Steps Checklist: Building Your Speaking Foundation

Creating a solid speaking foundation involves a systematic approach to developing your message, stories, content structure, and credibility. This detailed checklist will guide you through each step to ensure you build a compelling and effective speaking platform.

1. Message Development (TRUE Technique)

- **Target:**

  Identify a specific industry focus.

  Define the ideal audience role and position.

  List audience pain points.

  Specify company size and type.

  Test the target description with five industry professionals.

- **Rationale:**

  Research current industry trends.

  Identify urgent problems.

  Gather relevant statistics.

  Document the cost of inaction.

Create a compelling "why now" statement.

- **Uniqueness**:

    List your unique experiences.

    Document unusual methodologies.

    Identify your distinctive approach.

    Craft a unique positioning statement.

    Test differentiation with your target audience.

- **Expertise**:

    Include your degrees and certifications.

    Document your clients' results.

    Quantify your success.

    Site your publications.

    Create an expertise summary.

2. Story Development

- **Credential Story**:

    Write the first draft.

    Create multiple versions: 30 seconds, 2 minutes, and 5 minutes.

    Practice with a test audience. Record and critique delivery.

- **Connection Story**:

    Identify a relatable moment.

    Write the first draft.

    Add sensory details.

    Create multiple versions.

    Practice with a timer and get feedback from three people.

- **Change Story**:

    Document the transformation.

    Include specific results.

    Add emotional elements.

    Create versions for different lengths.

    Practice transitions and record to refine.

3. Content Architecture

- **Opening**:

    Create an attention-grabbing hook.

    Write a credibility statement.

    Develop a value proposition.

    Craft a connection moment.

- **Core Content**:

    Outline 3 main points.

    Develop supporting stories.

    Create action items.

    Design interaction points.

    Build in flexibility for audience engagement.

- **Closing**:

    Create a powerful ending.

    Develop a call to action.

    Write implementation steps.

    Craft a memorable final thought.

    Practice smooth transitions.

4. Credibility Building

- **Foundation Layer**:

    Update your professional bio.

    List all certifications.

    Document your speaking history.

    Create an experience summary.

    Organize your credentials.

- **Proof Layer:**

    Collect case studies.

    Gather testimonials.

    Document client results.

    Create a media kit.

    Organize success stories.

- **Authority Layer:**

    Join professional organizations.

    Seek board positions.

    Submit applications for awards.

    Build strategic partnerships.

Vincentism: You could have a food truck and get 1000 views on social media about it, but no one buys your food. Social media views don't always lead to paid engagements.

5. Testing and Refinement

Test the message with your target audience.

Practice stories with a timer.

Cut unnecessary content to increase efficiency.

Record your presentation and get professional feedback.

Write the minutes and seconds of each error from the recording

Update materials based on feedback.

Create a system to collect and analyze feedback consistently.

Practice your needed areas of improvement.

6. Documentation and Organization

Create a content folder system.

Organize all materials digitally.

Build a comprehensive presentation portfolio.

Establish reliable backup systems.

Set a schedule for regular updates.

Pro Tips:

Tackle one section at a time to avoid being overwhelmed.

Review the checklist monthly and update materials quarterly.

Regularly seek and incorporate feedback.

Track your progress consistently and celebrate even small victories.

> **Phipps Tip**: This checklist isn't just a one-off tool—it's a living document that should evolve as you grow in your speaking career. Regularly review and refine it to stay aligned with your goals and audience needs.

This comprehensive approach ensures that you build a robust speaking foundation that resonates with your audience, establishes your credibility, and enhances your professional growth.

Chapter 3: Crafting Your Speaking Topics and Content

Introduction

In the world of professional speaking, the selection and crafting of your topic are crucial. The success of your engagements largely hinges on how well your topics resonate with event planners and your target audience. This chapter provides a structured approach to creating speaking topics that are not only compelling but also marketable, ensuring they connect meaningfully with listeners and meet the specific needs of event organizers.

Section 3.1: Developing Your Topic Title

The Power of a Descriptive Title

A well-crafted title is your first impression: it can captivate potential clients and set the tone for your presentation. Titles like "Leadership Essentials" or "Pathways to Empowerment" are overly broad and do little to stand out in a crowded market. Instead, aim for clarity and specificity to grab attention and immediately convey the unique value of your talk.

Title Creation Guidelines

- **Be Specific and Descriptive**: Clearly articulate what your talk is about. Use precise language that reflects the depth and focus of your presentation.
- **Avoid Generic Terms Alone**: Generic terms can dilute the perceived value of your topic. Pair them with specific descriptors to enhance relevance and appeal.
- **Make the Benefit or Outcome Clear**: Your title should reflect the tangible value or transformation attendees can expect.
- **Consider Your Target Audience**: Tailor your title to resonate with the specific interests, needs, and professional language of your intended audience.
- **Keep It Memorable and Engaging**: A catchy, thought-provoking title can make your topic more memorable and increase the likelihood of engagement.

Customizing Titles for Different Audiences

Adapting your core topic to suit various audiences is a strategic way to increase your appeal and marketability. This customization shows that you understand and can address the unique challenges or interests of different groups.

Example: Base Topic: *"Communication with Less Confrontation"*

- **For Healthcare Professionals**: *"Navigating High Stakes: Effective Communication with Less Confrontation for Nurses"*
- **For IT Teams**: *"Bridging the Gap: Enhancing Team Communication with Less Confrontation for Technical Teams"*
- **For Educators**: *"Classroom Harmony: Fostering Constructive Communication with Less Confrontation"*

By modifying your base topic to fit different audience segments, you demonstrate a nuanced understanding of various professional environments, which can significantly boost your relevance and attractiveness as a speaker.

Theme Integration

Integrating specific themes into your speaking topics can not only align with event requirements but also enhance audience engagement by connecting more deeply with their interests and the event atmosphere.

Case Study 1: The Music-Themed Marketing Conference

Context: I faced a critical challenge when I was asked to present at the American Marketing Association's annual conference in Nashville, their theme was rock and roll.

Problem: I had overlooked the theme requirement, risking my professional reputation with a major client.

Solution: Acknowledging my mistake, I promptly contacted the conference coordinator to express my commitment to meeting their expectations. I then creatively integrated the rock and roll theme into my presentation title and content.

Creative Process:

- I brainstormed terms and concepts from rock and roll that could relate to public speaking. This process led me to focus on the common anxiety symptom of shaking, which many experience while speaking publicly.

- **Revised Title**: *"How to Take the Shake, Rattle, and Roll Out of Your Knees When Giving Presentations."* This title incorporated a well-known rock and roll song lyric while clearly communicating a benefit of this presentation—reducing public speaking anxiety that coincides with their theme.

Thematic Content Development:

- The following learning objectives were incorporated with this topic to provide development strategies during the presentation:
    - **Posture Exercise**: *"Blue Suede Shoes"* focused on proper foot positioning.
    - **Voice Modulation**: *"Jailhouse Rock"* engaged participants in improving their vocal delivery.
    - **Anxiety Management**: *"All Shook Up"* offered techniques to manage and reduce speaking anxiety.

Outcome: Attendees found value and enjoyment in this revised and customized theme. This decision led to additional bookings when the event organizer saw the creativity and adaptability.

Lessons Learned:

1. **Thorough Preparation**: Always read and understand all application requirements to avoid oversights that could jeopardize professional opportunities.

2. **Creative Adaptation**: View thematic requirements as opportunities to creatively enhance your presentation, rather than as constraints. This approach can lead to unique and memorable content that stands out.

Conclusion: This case study exemplifies how speakers can successfully integrate themes into their presentations, turning potential challenges into opportunities for enhanced engagement and business growth.

Case Study 2: Healthcare Symposium

Context: Margaret was invited to speak at a major healthcare symposium centered around the theme "Patient-Centered Care: Healing Beyond Medicine." Although she had a well-established workshop titled "Communication with Less Confrontation," it was not tailored to healthcare professionals, necessitating a significant adaptation to align with the symposium's focus.

Challenge

Margaret's primary challenge was to reframe her general communication workshop to meet the specific needs of healthcare professionals, who deal with high-stress situations involving patients and their families.

Process

1. **Research and Interviews**: Margaret started by interviewing healthcare professionals, including three nurses and a hospital administrator, to understand their unique communication challenges. This direct engagement helped her identify key issues such as managing emotional interactions and conveying difficult news under stress.
2. **Title and Content Customization**: From her research, Margaret developed the workshop title "Healing Words: Communication with Less Confrontation for Patient Care Excellence." This title not only tied into the symposium's theme but also clearly articulated the workshop's value proposition to healthcare professionals.
3. **Content Development**:
    - **Scenario-Specific Examples**: Margaret redesigned her teaching materials to reflect real hospital situations. Generic customer service scenarios were reworked into emergency room interactions and nurse-physician communication challenges.
    - **Practical Role-Plays**: She introduced role-playing exercises that had participants practice phrases and approaches for specific scenarios they frequently encountered, such as explaining delays or delivering bad news.
    - **Integration of Medical Context**: All examples and role-plays incorporated relevant medical terminology and

hospital protocols to ensure practical applicability.

Outcome

Margaret's session was met with enthusiastic feedback from participants, who felt that the content was uniquely relevant and directly applicable to their work environments. The organizer reported that her session received the highest evaluation scores at the symposium, particularly praising the deep integration of the theme into her presentation.

Follow-Up Success

The success of her tailored presentation led to six additional bookings at hospitals and medical conferences, accentuating the value of customized content for specialized audiences.

Lessons Learned

Margaret's experience highlights several key insights for professional speakers:

- **Thorough Audience Research**: Understanding the specific challenges and daily realities of your audience is crucial.
- **Beyond Surface-Level Changes**: Deep integration of the conference theme and audience-specific details into your presentation can significantly enhance its relevance and impact.
- **Feedback and Adaptation**: The positive feedback and subsequent bookings reinforced

the importance of tailoring presentations to meet the unique needs of specialized audiences.

Conclusion

This case study exemplifies how adapting a general workshop to fit a specialized theme and audience can transform a presentation from generic to extraordinary. Margaret's approach of thorough research, tailored content, and practical application provided immediate value to her audience and significantly boosted her professional reputation and opportunities within the healthcare industry.

Case Study 3: Tech Industry Conference

Context: Rebecca, an expert in leadership during organizational change, was invited to speak at TechForward, a prominent technology industry conference focused on "Innovation and Digital Transformation." Although her expertise was not directly related to technology, the principles she taught were universally applicable.

Challenge

Rebecca's challenge was to make her leadership content resonate with an audience deeply entrenched in the tech sector, which required a specific language and understanding of their environment.

Process

1. **Industry Research:** Rebecca immersed herself in technology industry publications to understand the language, priorities, and challenges specific to technology leaders.
2. **Content Reframing:**
    - Language Adaptation: Rebecca decided to reframe her leadership concepts using software development terminology, effectively "speaking their language."
    - Presentation Title: She rebranded her "Leadership in Challenging Times" talk to *"Debugging Leadership: Transforming Tech Teams Through Adaptive Management,"* incorporating key tech terms to attract interest.
3. **Deep Customization:**
    - Identifying Issues: Her section on pinpointing team issues was renamed *"Scanning for Bugs in Team Dynamics."*
    - Implementing Solutions: She described leadership strategies as *"Deploying New Leadership Protocols."*
    - Evaluating Results: The assessment phase was termed *"Testing and Iteration for Optimal Results."*
    - Continual Theme: Throughout her presentation, Rebecca used a consistent metaphor where leadership challenges were likened to "bugs," solutions to "patches," and ongoing improvements to "version updates."
4. **Relevant Examples:** She replaced generic case studies with specific examples from

well-known tech companies like Microsoft and Google, as well as insights from smaller tech startups, to illustrate her points effectively.

Outcome

Rebecca's presentation was highly engaging because it was tailored to the interests and language of the tech audience. Her approach demonstrated a deep understanding of their world, making her leadership principles more accessible and relevant.

Extended Opportunity

The success of her presentation led to an unexpected opportunity: the conference organizer offered Rebecca a chance to write a regular column for their industry publication, aimed at exploring leadership within the tech context.

Lessons Learned

- **Language Matters:** Using industry-specific language can transform general content into something that feels bespoke and deeply relevant.
- **Research is Key:** Understanding the audience's challenges, language, and culture through thorough research can guide effective content adaptation.
- **Metaphors Bridge Gaps:** Using metaphors relevant to the audience's field can make complex concepts more relatable and memorable.

Conclusion

This case study shows how well-researched leadership principles can be tailored to any industry. Rebecca's integration of tech language and examples increased her relevance and created new professional opportunities, demonstrating how targeted content adaptation expands influence in specialized fields.

Vincentism: Everybody wants apple pie but nobody wants to plant apple seeds.

Practical Exercise: Theme Integration Workshop

Core Presentation Title: *"Maximizing Team Efficiency: Strategies for Streamlined Success"*

Theme 1: Sustainability/Green Business

- **Adapted Title**: *"Green Efficiency: Sustainable Strategies for Eco-Friendly Team Success"*
- **Supporting Activity**: Conduct a *"Green Brainstorming Session"* where participants identify current practices in their workflow that impact the environment negatively and brainstorm sustainable alternatives.
- **Content Modification**: For this version, the presentation would emphasize how sustainable practices can not only help save the

environment but also enhance team efficiency by reducing waste and costs. Examples would include case studies from companies that have successfully integrated green technologies and processes. These would demonstrate tangible benefits like reduced energy costs and enhanced corporate reputation.

Theme 2: Digital Revolution

- **Adapted Title:** *"Digitizing Team Efficiency: Leveraging Technology for Streamlined Success"*
- **Supporting Activity:** Facilitate a "Tech Tool Speed Dating" session where participants rotate through stations to quickly learn and evaluate different digital tools that could enhance their team's efficiency.
- **Content Modification:** This presentation will focus on how digital tools and technologies can streamline team operations and improve communication. Content would be adapted to include discussions on the latest digital trends such as AI, blockchain, and cloud computing. Real-world examples of teams that have transformed their processes through digital solutions would be highlighted to show the impact of tech adoption on efficiency.

Theme 3: Post-Pandemic Workplace

- **Adapted Title:** *"Remote Efficiency: Building High-Performing Teams in the Post-Pandemic Workplace"*
- **Supporting Activity:** Host a "Remote Office Olympics" where participants engage in a

series of fun, collaborative tasks that can be done remotely to build team spirit and improve remote collaboration.
- **Content Modification**: The focus here would be on strategies for maintaining and enhancing team efficiency when working remotely. The presentation would include best practices for virtual collaboration, maintaining team morale, and managing remote workflows. It would also address common challenges faced by teams in the post-pandemic era, such as digital fatigue and communication barriers, providing practical solutions to overcome them.

Conclusion: These themed adaptations not only tailor the core presentation to different audiences but also enrich the content with specific, actionable insights relevant to each theme. This approach ensures that the presentation remains fresh and highly relevant, increasing engagement and applicability for diverse audiences.

Section 3.2: Content Summary Development

Purpose of the Content Summary

The content summary acts as a concise tool for capturing the essence of your presentation. It serves the following functions: informs potential attendees about the relevance of your topic, outlines the key problems it addresses, details what participants will learn, and explains how it will benefit them. This summary is often a factor in whether someone chooses to attend your session or further engage with your content.

Writing an Effective Summary

An effective content summary is crafted to grab attention and make a clear case for the value of your presentation. Here's how to write one:

1. **Address Specific Pain Points**: Identify and articulate the specific challenges or problems your audience faces that your presentation will address. This connection personalizes the summary for your audience, making the content relevant.
2. **Highlight Unique Approaches**: Mention any novel methods, frameworks, or perspectives you will use. This not only sets your presentation apart from others but also signals to your audience that they can expect new insights.
3. **Include Concrete Outcomes**: Be explicit about what attendees will take away from your session. Whether it's skills, knowledge, strategies, or specific tools, make sure these outcomes are tangible and desirable.
4. **Be Clear and Concise**: Keep your summary within 100-200 words, ensuring the message is succinct. Clarity and brevity are key to maintaining the reader's attention and interest.
5. **Avoid Jargon**: Unless you are presenting for a niche audience that expects and understands industry-specific language, keep your

summary free of jargon. This makes your content accessible to a broader audience.

Example Content Summary

Presentation Title Content Summary: In today's rapidly evolving digital landscape, traditional leadership strategies often fall short in sparking true innovation. This presentation delves into why contemporary leadership is pivotal and the specific challenges it addresses, such as navigating digital transformation and fostering a culture of innovation. Participants will learn cutting-edge leadership frameworks tailored to the digital age, gain practical tools for implementing change, and discover strategies to inspire and manage creative teams effectively. This session promises not only to enhance your leadership skills but also to equip you with the ability to directly influence your organization's innovative capabilities, driving tangible improvements in performance and competitiveness.

This summary clearly outlines the importance of the topic, addresses common pain points in leadership during digital transformation, highlights unique, actionable strategies, and promises concrete benefits for the audience, making it an effective tool for attracting attendees.

Case Study: Evolution of a Content Summary

Background: Camille, an experienced speaker, faced rejection from the Regional Leadership Summit due to a lackluster content summary in her presentation proposal. The feedback highlighted a need for greater specificity and clarity to meet attendee expectations.

Initial Challenge

Camille's original summary was too generic, filled with clichés, and lacked the distinct value proposition needed to stand out:

- **Original Summary**: "A motivational presentation about overcoming challenges and achieving success through perseverance and determination. This inspirational talk will help attendees reach their goals and become better leaders in today's fast-paced world."

This summary failed to convey the unique aspects of her presentation or how it would specifically benefit the attendees, making it indistinguishable from many others.

Process of Revision

Prompted by the committee's feedback and guided by advice from her mentor, Camille undertook a detailed revision of her summary:

1. **Audience Identification**: She pinpointed the specific audience—mid-level managers aspiring to senior roles.
2. **Strategy Articulation**: She clearly outlined the evidence-based strategies her talk would cover.

3. **Concrete Outcomes**: She specified what attendees would learn and how they could apply these lessons.
4. **Feedback Incorporation**: Camille sought input from colleagues to refine her summary further.

Revised Summary

The new summary she crafted was tailored to reflect the needs of her audience and the unique insights she could provide:

- **Revised Summary**: Drawing from two decades of research and real-world experience, this dynamic session equips mid-level managers with practical strategies for navigating organizational change. Participants will learn a proven four-step framework for leading teams through transitions, backed by case studies from Fortune 500 companies. This presentation includes interactive exercises that allow managers to apply concepts to their current challenges, specifically addressing resistance management, communication protocols, and performance maintenance during periods of uncertainty. Attendees will leave with a digital toolkit containing assessment instruments, implementation guides, and a 30-day action plan customized to their organization's needs.

Outcome

The revised summary was a success, leading not only to her acceptance into the conference but also an upgrade to a featured speaker slot. The selection committee recognized the tangible value her presentation promised, which was now clearly communicated in her summary.

Lessons Learned

- **Specificity Sells**: Camille learned that specificity in content summaries is crucial. Event planners and attendees are looking for clear, actionable value that can be directly applied to their professional challenges.
- **Template Development**: Post-rejection, Camille developed a detailed template for her summaries, which she customizes for each event to ensure clarity and relevance.
- **Professional Growth**: The initial rejection served as a pivotal learning experience for Camille, underscoring the importance of clear communication in marketing her speaking engagements.

Conclusion

Camille's experience illustrates the critical role of a content summary in securing speaking engagements. A well-crafted summary must highlight the speaker's unique approach, the practical value of the content, and how it addresses the specific needs of the audience. This case study serves as a valuable blueprint for speakers on how to effectively communicate their value proposition through a content summary.

Practical Exercise: Content Summary Development

This exercise helps refine your ability to create effective content summaries that communicate the specific value of your presentation. Follow the steps below to craft a summary that resonates clearly with different audience segments.

Initial Draft

Task: Write a first draft of your content summary focusing on a hypothetical presentation titled *"Revolutionizing Team Collaboration with Advanced Digital Tools."*

Initial Draft: Discover the secrets to enhancing team collaboration in today's fast-paced work environment. This presentation will explore innovative tools and strategies that help leaders and teams achieve greater success and efficiency. Attendees will leave equipped to implement these solutions and drive significant improvements in their workplace dynamics.

Specificity Challenge

1. **Circle Generic Terms or Buzzwords**: Secrets, success, innovative, significant improvements
2. **Highlight Specific Outcomes or Benefits**: Achieve greater efficiency, equipped to implement solutions

Refined Summary: Learn how to enhance team collaboration with specific digital tools that increase project completion rates by 29%. This presentation will detail targeted strategies and software solutions designed to streamline communication and task management among team members. Attendees will gain hands-on experience with these tools, enabling them to boost operational efficiency and reduce project timelines in their organizations.

Audience Adaptation

Adapted and refined summaries for different audience segments:

1. **C-level Executives**: Explore strategic digital solutions that drive a 29% improvement in project efficiency across your organization. This session provides an executive overview of cutting-edge tools that enhance decision-making and optimize team collaboration. Gain insights into integrating these technologies to scale business operations and achieve measurable outcomes in productivity and revenue growth.
2. **Front-line Managers**: Master practical digital tools that can immediately enhance your team's productivity by reducing project completion times. This workshop focuses on easy-to-implement software that improves daily communication and task management, directly addressing common operational challenges faced by managers. Participants will learn to deploy these tools to elevate team performance and meet key operational targets.
3. **Non-profit Organizations**: This presentation delves into cost-effective digital tools that non-profit managers can utilize to enhance

team collaboration and increase project output by 29%. Learn to leverage budget-friendly technologies that maximize resource efficiency and improve team coordination, crucial for mission-driven success and impact.
4. **Technical Professionals**: Deep dive into advanced digital tools that can transform how your technical teams collaborate, leading to a 29% increase in efficiency. This session will cover specialized software that supports complex project management and enhances communication among diverse technical stakeholders. Participants will explore practical applications of these tools, tailored to high-stakes technical environments.

Peer Review

Task: Exchange the adapted summaries with a colleague.

Feedback Goals:

- Identify the main problem being solved.
- Confirm the summary is tailored to the specific audience.
- Highlight the concrete benefits mentioned.
- Point out any vague language that remains.

Key Components to Review:

- **Problem Statement**: Have a clearly defined issue that the presentation addresses.
- **Solution Overview**: Describe what will be covered to address the problem.

- **Methodology Highlight**: Mention specific methods or technologies that will be used.
- **Benefit Statement**: Identify concrete benefits attendees will attain.
- **Credibility Elements**: Align the presenter's expertise or evidence supporting the content.

Conclusion: This exercise not only sharpens your content summary writing skills but also ensures that your presentations are tailored effectively. This will help to meet the needs and expectations of diverse audiences, enhancing the impact and relevance of your professional speaking engagements.

Section 3.3: Creating Learning Objectives

Creating effective learning objectives is crucial for the success of any educational presentation. These objectives not only guide your content creation process but also help your audience understand what they will gain by participating. Here's how to craft objectives that are clear, actionable, and directly tied to the needs of your audience.

Characteristics of Strong Learning Objectives

1. **Start with Action Verbs**: Use strong, clear action verbs to begin each objective, which helps specify what attendees will do or achieve.
2. **Keep Them Concise**: Limit objectives to 10 words or fewer to ensure they are to the point and easy to remember.

3. **Focus on Achievable Outcomes**: Objectives should be realistic and achievable within the scope of your presentation.
4. **Be Specific and Measurable**: Avoid ambiguity. Clarify how success is evaluated.
5. **Align with Content Delivery**: Ensure that each objective is directly related to the content you are presenting and that you have the resources and time to cover it effectively.

Action Verbs to Use

- **Identify**: Learn to recognize specific information, concepts, or tools.
- **Demonstrate**: Show how to use a skill or concept in a scenario.
- **Apply**: Use knowledge or techniques in practical and relevant situations.
- **Analyze**: Break down a concept or problem to understand its components.
- **Develop**: Build or create something from the information provided.
- **Implement**: Put plans, strategies, or theories into action.
- **Recognize**: Acknowledge or distinguish critical elements or patterns.
- **Utilize**: Make use of methods, tools, or concepts effectively.

What to Avoid In Learning Objectives

- **Vague Promises**: Prevent ambiguity by being specific about what content will be covered; they need to promise specific skills or knowledge.

- **Unmeasurable Outcomes**: Avoid objectives that can't be quantified or assessed.
- **Results You Can't Control**: Ensure that the objectives depend on the content provided and activities planned, not external factors.
- **Overly Complex Statements**: Keep objectives simple and straightforward to avoid confusion.
- **Personal Interpretations**: Use quantifiable data with measurable results, not subject to individual interpretation.

Examples

- **Poor Objective**: *"Attendees will become successful leaders."*
    - **Better Objective**: *"Identify three key leadership strategies that can enhance team performance."*
- **Poor Objective**: *"Learn everything about conflict resolution."*
    - **Better Objective**: *"Apply two techniques that can build rapport and accountability."*

By following these guidelines, you ensure that your learning objectives are a valuable tool for both you and your audience. They help participants gauge what they will learn and allow you to focus your presentation on delivering tangible, useful outcomes.

Case Study: Healthcare Conference Learning Objectives

Background: *Ron wanted to develop a keynote on how companies can make a positive impact on reducing waste.*

Initial Problem

He felt his content was too preachy and was too specific to deliver to the masses. Initially, Ron wanted to only speak at environmental conferences or conventions focusing on climate change and control.

Feedback and Revision

The conference coordinator informed Michael that the objectives needed to explicitly state what attendees would be able to do as a result of the session, emphasizing the need for actionable and observable outcomes.

Revised Objectives

After Ron and I incorporated the TRUE Technique, we later identified that his message was to really encourage others to take the steps to make their environment better. We developed principles of growth, engagement, and preparation. I worked with Ron to establish foundational principles. We started with how he started an effort of planting seeds. We then looked at how he was able to engage local community leaders for support. We then identified steps that schools, programs, and companies could take to support the healthy planet efforts.

- **Identify** the environment in which a business must have to grow.
- **Demonstrate** like seeds to begin thinking about your business.
- **Apply** a framework based on a seed and planting metaphor to grow your business.

These revised objectives were:

- **Action-Oriented**: Each began with a verb that implied clear action participants would take.
- **Specific and Measurable**: They detailed precisely what attendees would learn and be able to implement.
- **Observable**: Each objective focused on skills that could be demonstrated and observed during the session.

Outcome

Ron grew this effort from a local staff of six into an international staff of 50 - 60. We parlayed the principles of growth to first begin making subtle and less noticeable changes in yourself and your surroundings. We then looked at how engagement is indicative of how communication and leadership impact the conveyance of messages. We concluded that preparing for changes and adapting accordingly is a model everyone should follow by knowing your goals, but still being flexible enough to adapt.

The revised objectives were quickly approved by the conference committee, which also used them as examples for other speakers to follow. This change not only facilitated the acceptance of his session but also enhanced the structure and delivery of his presentation. Michael was able to focus his presentation more effectively, developing exercises that aligned directly with each objective.

Impact on Presentation

By aligning his presentation content with these clear, specific objectives, Michael ensured that the participants had a practical and applicable learning experience. Attendees explicitly appreciated the tangible skills they acquired, which was reflected in their positive feedback and high ratings for the session.

Long-Term Changes

This experience profoundly influenced Michael's approach to creating presentation content. He now uses a "verb bank" to ensure that his learning objectives are always action-oriented and appropriate for the intended learning level. This systematic approach helps him design his presentations to deliver concrete value, improving both participant satisfaction and his effectiveness as an educator.

Conclusion

These revised principles were modified to address leaders in corporate environments because the new keynote was not just about impacting the planet, but about applying principles that impact the people.

Dr. Michael Rivera's experience underscores the importance of well-crafted learning objectives in the success of educational presentations. Clear, specific, and measurable objectives not only facilitate conference approval but also guide the creation of focused, impactful content that directly addresses the needs of the audience. This case study serves as a valuable lesson for all professionals in the field of education and training, highlighting the need to think from the perspective of participants and event planners when designing learning experiences.

Practical Exercise: Learning Objectives Workshop

This comprehensive exercise helps refine your approach to crafting effective learning objectives for presentations across various contexts. Follow the steps to enhance the precision and impact of your training or speaking engagements.

The Verb Challenge

Task: Choose 10 action verbs that apply to your topic. For instance, if your topic is "Digital Marketing Strategies," relevant verbs could include:

1. Analyze
2. Construct
3. Design
4. Evaluate
5. Implement
6. Optimize
7. Create
8. Test
9. Measure
10. Customize

Objective Creation: Use each verb to create a specific learning objective. Examples might be:

1. Analyze current digital marketing trends to identify opportunities for growth.
2. Construct a content calendar that aligns with seasonal marketing peaks.
3. Design a user-friendly landing page for campaign conversions.
4. Evaluate the effectiveness of different social media platforms for targeted ads.
5. Implement SEO best practices in website updates.
6. Optimize email marketing strategies to increase open rates.
7. Create engaging content that enhances brand visibility.

8. Test A/B variations of email campaigns to determine the most effective format.
9. Measure the ROI of digital campaigns using analytics tools.
10. Customize digital advertisements to appeal to different demographic segments.

Now You Try: After you create your own objectives, have a colleague check each objective to ensure it is specific, measurable, and clearly defined.

The Specificity Test

Task: Write three distinct learning objectives for your presentation. For each objective, critically evaluate:

1. **Can this be measured?** Ensure there is a clear metric or indicator for success.
2. **Can I guarantee this outcome?** Confirm that the objective is realistic and under your control.
3. **Is it achievable in the time allotted?** Consider whether the objective can realistically be met within the duration of your session.
4. **Does it align with my content?** Make sure the objective directly relates to your presentation content.

Audience Level Adaptation

Task: Select one of your learning objectives and adapt it for different audience skill levels. Examples:

- **Beginners**: "Identify basic SEO tactics that can improve website visibility."

- **Intermediate learners**: "Implement advanced SEO strategies to enhance site ranking and user engagement."
- **Advanced practitioners**: "Evaluate and optimize an existing SEO strategy to maximize search engine results page (SERP) positioning."

Note: Observe how the action verb and the level of detail change to suit each audience's experience level.

Time-Based Objective Setting

Task: Create learning objectives tailored to the length of the presentation. Examples:

- **A 30-minute keynote**: "Introduce the core principles of digital marketing and their importance in the current market."
- **A 90-minute workshop**: "Guide participants through the creation of a digital marketing plan, including goal setting, platform selection, and basic content strategy."
- **A half-day seminar**: "Conduct an in-depth analysis of digital marketing techniques, practice comprehensive campaign planning, and perform hands-on activities with real-time feedback."

Explanation: The depth and scope of each objective expand with the available time, allowing for a more detailed exploration of the topic in longer sessions.

Conclusion

This structured approach to developing learning objectives ensures that your educational content is targeted, measurable, and adapted to meet the needs of your audience effectively. By considering these factors, you can maximize the impact of your presentations and ensure meaningful learning experiences for your participants.

Section 3.4: Professional Bio Development

Creating a professional bio is essential for speakers as it introduces you to your audience and establishes your credibility before you even begin your presentation. Crafting three distinct versions of your bio ensures that you have an appropriate format for different contexts, such as conference brochures, event websites, or promotional materials.

The Three-Version Approach

1. **Short Version (50 words or less):**
   - **Purpose:** Ideal for quick introductions, social media profiles, or as part of a larger speaker list.
   - **Content:** Focus on your core expertise and main achievement or role.
2. **Standard Version (100 words or less):**
   - **Purpose:** Suitable for event programs, professional networking sites like

LinkedIn, or detailed speaker introductions.
   - **Content**: Include your expertise, key credentials, a notable achievement, and how your work benefits your target audience.
3. **Full Version (250 words or less)**:
   - **Purpose**: Perfect for your website, guest blog bios, or extended speaker profiles at conferences.
   - **Content**: Expand on your expertise, detailed credentials, multiple achievements, audience benefits, a personal touch that connects you to your subject, and a call to action.

Elements to Include

1. **Relevant Expertise**:
   - Highlight the specific areas of your professional expertise that are relevant to your speaking topics.
2. **Credentials**:
   - Mention your academic degrees, certifications, or other professional qualifications that establish your credibility in your field.
3. **Notable Achievements**:
   - Include awards, recognitions, major projects, or publications that can showcase your success and impact in your industry.
4. **Target Audience Benefits**:
   - Explain how your work or insights benefit your audience, tailoring this

section to reflect the needs or interests of your typical audience.
5. **Personal Touch:**
   - Add a personal element that makes your bio relatable—this could be a brief mention of a hobby, a personal motivation, or a unique aspect of your professional journey.
6. **Call to Action:**
   - End with an encouragement for the reader to engage with your work further, whether it's visiting your website, following you on social media, or contacting you for more information.

Example Bios

Short Version: 50 Words (367 Characters)

Vincent Phipps is a keynote speaker, author, and owner of Communication VIP. Vincent is in the top 1% of experts addressing interpersonal impact and emotional adaptation. His presentations are filled with energy, expertise, and engagement. Vincent develops strategic alliances with companies and conferences to amplify relationships and revenue.

Standard Version: 93 Words (726 Characters)

Vincent Phipps is in the top 1% of experts specializing in communication, communication, and leadership. Vincent owns Communication VIP, which is a consulting company in Chattanooga, Tennessee.

Vincent is the author of "*Lead Out Loud*" and "*Um-believable Public Speaking*". Vincent and his company provide strategies to conferences, companies, and organizations wanting to influence and lead by increasing communication efficiency. Vincent's presentations are always filled with energy, engagement, and expertise. Vincent's doctoral dissertation (2026) recognizes that the synergy between interpersonal communication and emotional intelligence are the most significant factors determining leadership success for today's professionals.

Full Version: 225 Words (1,589 Characters)

Vincent Phipps is in the top 1% of experts specializing in communication, communication, and leadership. Vincent owns Communication VIP which is a consulting company in Chattanooga, Tennessee. Vincent is the author of "*Lead Out Loud*" and "*Um-believable Public Speaking*". Vincent and his company provide strategies to conferences, companies, and organizations wanting to influence and lead by increasing communication efficiency. Vincent's presentations are always filled with energy, engagement, and expertise. Vincent's doctoral dissertation (2026) recognizes that the synergy between interpersonal communication and emotional intelligence are the most significant factors determining leadership success for today's professionals. In 2007, Vincent survived a nearly fatal car accident. He broke his neck in two places and his skull was split open. During his recovery, Vincent was inspired to use his communication skills to provide strategies for others dealing with professional and personal challenges. Vincent founded Communication VIP Training and Coaching. Vincent has delivered over 4,000 paid presentations. Vincent was awarded the CSP (Certified Speaking Professional) certification, which is the highest earned honor by the National Speakers Association. Vincent is certified in DiSC, MBTI, and Behavioral Psychology. Vincent blends energy, expertise, humor, and interaction to keep his audience laughing and learning. Vincent's presentation philosophy is *"If I can get you to laugh, I can get you to listen. If I can get you to listen, I can help your communication skills amplify!"*

These bio versions effectively communicate Jane's qualifications and relevance to different platforms, ensuring that her professional introduction is always tailored and impactful.

Bio Examples

The Journey to an Effective Speaker Bio: Margaret's Story

Challenge: Margaret needed to submit a speaker bio in three different lengths for an upcoming domestic violence awareness conference, a task that proved more challenging than anticipated. Her initial attempt at a comprehensive 400-word bio was difficult to scale down effectively.

Solution Process

Mentor's Advice: Margaret was advised to start with the shortest version first, focusing on the essentials, and then expanding for the longer versions. This approach ensures clarity and consistency across all versions.

Bio Versions

1. **Short Bio (30 words)**:
    - Margaret Williams empowers survivors of domestic violence with evidence-based resilience training. A certified trauma counselor, she brings 15 years of dedicated advocacy and experience.
2. **Standard Bio (90 words)**:
    - Margaret Williams transforms domestic violence discussions through her 'Pivot Point' methodology. Founder of Pivot Point Chattanooga and a certified trauma counselor, she has guided over 1,000 survivors towards rebuilding their lives. With 15 years of front-line experience, Margaret combines clinical expertise with compassionate storytelling in her impactful presentations. Her work, featured in leading advocacy journals, also includes training crisis intervention teams nationally. She holds advanced certifications in trauma-informed care and is a board member of the National Coalition Against Domestic Violence.

3. **Full Bio (150 words):**
    - Margaret Williams is a pioneering advocate in domestic violence support, introducing the transformative 'Pivot Point' methodology. As the founder of Pivot Point Chattanooga, she has committed 15 years to empowering survivors to reclaim their futures. A certified trauma counselor and crisis intervention specialist, Margaret has supported over 1,000 survivors through their healing journeys. Her unique, evidence-based approach merges clinical expertise with heartfelt storytelling, making her a sought-after speaker at national conferences and training programs. Margaret's contributions have been highlighted in top advocacy publications, and she regularly conducts training for crisis teams across the US. She holds advanced certifications in trauma-informed care and serves on the board of the National Coalition Against Domestic Violence. Margaret's sessions provide professionals with actionable strategies and inspire survivors with renewed hope. Contact Margaret to bring her transformative insights to your next event.

Outcomes

The conference organizers used Margaret's bios effectively across various platforms—short bio for the mobile app, standard for the printed program, and full version on the website. This strategic use of different bio lengths ensured that her professional image was consistently presented, regardless of the medium.

Reflection

Margaret found that creating different versions of her bio was not only necessary for meeting specific content length requirements but also invaluable for maintaining a cohesive professional image across all her engagements. She now uses these versions consistently, which saves time and enhances her presentation of a unified image.

Key Takeaway

Margaret's approach emphasizes the importance of starting with a concise core of your professional identity and then building outward with additional details as needed for longer formats. This method ensures that all essential information is included in even the shortest bio, while longer versions build on this foundation to provide a more comprehensive view of her expertise and contributions.

When writing professional bios, especially for speakers who need to engage and captivate diverse audiences, following strategic guidelines ensures each bio version effectively communicates your expertise and appeal. Here are refined tips to help craft compelling bios across different lengths:

1. Build on Each Version

Start with a concise base in the short bio and expand details progressively in the standard and full versions. Ensure key messages are consistent across all versions to maintain a coherent professional narrative.

2. Maintain a Professional Yet Personal Tone

While the tone should remain professional, adding a personal touch helps differentiate you from others. This could be a brief mention of a passion, a unique perspective on your field, or an anecdote that relates to your professional journey.

3. Incorporate Specific Numbers and Achievements

Concrete achievements, such as "increased sales by 24%" or "trained over 500 professionals," provide tangible evidence of your success and expertise. These specifics add credibility and allow the audience to gauge the impact of your work.

4. Highlight Relevant Certifications and Affiliations

Include certifications, degrees, or memberships relevant to your field to enhance credibility. This not only showcases your commitment to professional development but also assures the audience of your qualifications.

5. Focus on How You Serve Your Audience

Clearly articulate the benefits your audience will gain from your presentations. Whether it's learning new skills, gaining unique insights, or receiving practical tools, make sure your bio addresses how you add value to your audience.

6. Use Active Voice and Dynamic Verbs

Active voice and dynamic verbs convey confidence and drive. Phrases like "deliver powerful solutions," "transform business practices," or "lead innovative projects" demonstrate action and impact, energizing your bio.

7. Craft a Clear, Non-Pushy Call to Action

End with a subtle call to action that invites the audience to learn more about you or engage with your content. Whether it's visiting a website, connecting on social media, or contacting you for more details, ensure it feels natural and not overly promotional.

Using these guidelines will help ensure that your bio is not only informative and professionally appealing but also engaging and personal, making you stand out as a speaker.

Practical Exercise: Bio Development

This exercise guides you through the development of three key versions of a professional bio. Follow each step carefully to craft a bio that effectively communicates your expertise and credentials.

Write Your Short Bio

Content	Example
Core Expertise	- Digital Marketing Specialist - Book Editing Strategist - Web Design Architect
Target Audience	- Small to mid-sized business owners - HR professionals - Accounting Executives
Methodology	- ROI-driven marketing strategies - TRUE Presentation strategies - SMART Goals

Credentials	<ul><li>Industry Certification</li><li>PhD</li><li>Author of...</li></ul>

Short Bio: John Smith is a Google Analytics Certified Digital Marketing Specialist, known for his ROI-driven strategies tailored specifically for small to mid-sized businesses.

Expand to Standard Bio

1. **Add Specific Achievements**: Increased client revenue by an average of 39% within the first six months.
2. **Include Relevant Credentials**: MBA in Marketing from NYU Stern School of Business
3. **Mention Key Audiences You Serve**: Retail and E-commerce sectors
4. **Add Industry Recognition**: Featured in *'Marketing Weekly'*
5. **End with a Clear Expertise Statement**: Expert in translating data analytics into actionable growth plans for diverse markets.

Standard Bio: John Smith is a Google Analytics Certified Digital Marketing Specialist with an MBA from NYU Stern, specializing in ROI-driven strategies that have notably increased client revenue by 39% on average within six months. With a focus on the retail and e-commerce sectors, John applies his expertise to transform data insights into actionable growth plans. His innovative approach has been featured in *'Marketing Weekly,'* and he is recognized as a leading expert in digital marketing for diverse markets.

Create Full Bio

1. **Develop Compelling Opening**: John Smith is at the forefront of digital marketing innovation...
2. **Add Professional Journey Highlights**: Eleven years of experience scaling startups to established enterprises...
3. **Include Methodology Details**: Specializes in leveraging advanced analytics to optimize marketing spend...
4. **Mention Significant Projects/Clients**: Worked with Fortune 500 clients like TechForward and EcoGear...
5. **Add Personal Mission**: Committed to helping businesses achieve sustainable growth through data-driven insights...
6. **Close with Call to Action**: Connect with John to revolutionize your marketing strategy at www.johnsmithmarketing.com.

Full Bio: John Smith is at the forefront of digital marketing innovation, leveraging 11 years of experience from scaling startups to established enterprises. As a Google Analytics Certified expert with an MBA from NYU Stern, he specializes in developing ROI-driven marketing strategies, which have increased client revenue by 39% within six months. John's approach to using advanced analytics to optimize marketing spend has benefited notable clients like TechForward and EcoGear. Featured in

'Marketing Weekly,' he is recognized for translating complex data into actionable growth plans. Committed to sustainable business growth, John empowers retail and e-commerce leaders to exceed their marketing goals. For a tailored strategy that drives real results, visit John at www.johnsmithmarketing.com.

Review and Refine

1. **Check Word Count of Each Version**: Ensure short bio is around 30 words, standard bio around 90 words, and full bio around 150 words.
2. **Verify Consistency Across Versions**: Key facts and themes should align and reflect the same professional image.
3. **Ensure All Claims Are Verifiable**: Credentials, achievements, and recognitions should be accurate and truthful.
4. **Test Readability Aloud**: This helps catch any awkward phrasing or errors.
5. **Get Feedback from Colleagues**: Use their insights to refine and polish each version.

By meticulously crafting each version of your bio, you can ensure a cohesive and compelling professional narrative that resonates with your audience and effectively highlights your expertise and unique contributions.

Key Takeaways & Action Items

Your ability to craft compelling speaking content is crucial to establishing your authority and engaging your audience. Here's a structured approach to refine your materials for optimal impact:

Key Takeaways:

1. **Topic Title Specificity**:
    - Ensure your topic title is specific, descriptive, and immediately communicates the value and focus of your presentation.
2. **Content Summary Clarity**:
    - Your content summary should succinctly convey the importance of your topic, what the audience will learn, and how it will benefit them, using specific and measurable terms.
3. **Learning Objectives Precision**:
    - Learning objectives should be actionable, achievable, and measurable. They must articulate the skills or knowledge the audience will gain.
4. **Versatile Professional Bios**:
    - Maintain three versions of your professional bio to cater to different platforms and needs, ensuring each is consistent in messaging but appropriate in length and detail.
5. **Audience Customization**:
    - Tailor your content to resonate with your specific audience, taking into

account their expertise level, industry, and unique challenges.

Action Items:

1. **Create Three Versions of Your Topic Title**:
    - Develop three different iterations of your topic title for varying contexts, each increasingly detailed but always clear and focused.
2. **Write a 150-Word Content Summary**:
    - Craft a content summary that outlines the key points of your presentation, its relevance, the audience's takeaways, and potential impacts on their professional or personal growth.
3. **Develop 3-5 Specific Learning Objectives**:
    - Formulate 3-5 learning objectives using strong action verbs. These should state what the attendees will learn and how they can apply this knowledge practically.
4. **Draft Your Three Bio Versions**:
    - Prepare three lengths of your professional bio: a 30-word short version, a 90-word standard version, and a 150-word full version, each expanding on the last but consistently reflecting your professional identity.
5. **Test Your Content with a Peer Group**:
    - Present your developed content to a peer group or mentors for feedback. Focus on the clarity, relevance, and engagement of your topic title, summary, learning objectives, and bios.

Reminder:

Your speaking content is indeed your product—treat it as such by investing the necessary time and effort into its development and refinement. This approach ensures that your presentations meet professional standards and effectively address the needs and expectations of your audience. By consistently reviewing and updating your materials based on feedback and evolving expertise, you maintain relevance and effectiveness in your professional speaking engagements.

Chapter 4: Finding Speaking Opportunities

Introduction

For professional speakers, finding the right opportunities is essential to building a successful career. This chapter provides a systematic approach to identifying, evaluating, and pursuing speaking engagements. These engagements not only align with your expertise but also support your career goals. Whether you're just starting out or looking to expand your reach, understanding where and how to find these opportunities can significantly impact your professional trajectory.

Understanding Types of Speaking Events

The speaking circuit offers a variety of platforms and audiences. Knowing the different types of events can help you tailor your content and proposals to suit specific venues and audience needs.

Conference Types

- **Professional Association Conferences**: These events are ideal for networking and showcasing expertise within a specific professional community. They include:
    - Industry-specific gatherings
    - Annual meetings
    - Regional chapters
    - National conventions
- **Example**: Speaking at an annual meeting for the American Marketing Association.
- **Corporate Events**: Companies often host events to enhance the skills of their employees or to foster leadership qualities. Opportunities include:
    - Leadership training
    - Professional development workshops
    - Team building sessions
    - Sales meetings
- **Example**: Delivering a workshop on effective team communication at a corporate retreat.
- **Educational Institutions**: These venues are perfect for educational or motivational topics aimed at students or professional development for educators. They include:
    - Universities
    - Professional schools

- - Training programs
  - Educational conferences
- **Example**: Conducting a seminar on career development at a university or speaking at a conference focused on innovations in education.
- **Non-Profit Organizations**: Nonprofits host a variety of events that can benefit from expert speakers, particularly those who can speak to the organization's mission or help raise awareness and funds. Events might include:
  - Fundraising events
  - Awareness campaigns
  - Volunteer training sessions
  - Annual meetings
- **Example**: Leading a session on community engagement strategies during a non-profit's annual meeting.

Evaluating and Pursuing Opportunities

To effectively pursue speaking opportunities, consider the following steps:

1. **Research Events**: Look for events that align with your expertise and speaking goals. Use resources like industry newsletters, professional associations, and networking groups to find opportunities.
2. **Evaluate Fit**: Assess whether the event's audience, size, and theme align with your

speaking style and content. Ensure that the event will effectively showcase your expertise and contribute to your career goals.
3. **Prepare Proposals**: Tailor your proposals to each opportunity, highlighting how your topic will add value to the event and resonate with the audience. Include a clear title, a compelling summary, and outlined objectives.
4. **Network**: Build relationships with event organizers, previous speakers, and attendees to improve your chances of being selected. Networking can also provide insider insights into what each event is looking for in a speaker.
5. **Follow Up**: After submitting a proposal, follow up with the organizers to express your enthusiasm about the opportunity and to offer any additional information that might help them consider you as their future speaker.
6. **Leverage Every Speaking Engagement**: After each event, ask for feedback, gather testimonials, and request recordings of your session to use as promotional material for future opportunities.

Conclusion

Finding and securing the right speaking opportunities requires careful planning and persistence. By understanding the various types of events and how to effectively approach each, you can significantly enhance your visibility and impact as a professional speaker. Remember, every event is a chance to grow your network, refine your speaking skills, and build your reputation in the industry.

Finding Speaking Opportunities

Expanding your speaking career involves more than just honing your presentation skills; it also requires effective strategies for discovering and seizing speaking opportunities. Here's how you can approach lead generation, build relationships, and leverage existing connections to find valuable speaking engagements.

Lead Generation Sources

1. Professional Lead Services

- **Paid speaking opportunity databases**: Paid lead generator subscriptions provide searchable databases of speaking opportunities that can be filtered by location, topic, or event type.
- **Industry newsletters**: Subscribe to newsletters from within your industry to stay updated on upcoming conferences and events.
- **Speaker bureaus**: These organizations represent speakers and help match them with speaking opportunities. Joining a bureau can significantly increase your exposure to potential clients.

- **Conference listings**: Websites such as AllConferences.com or ConferenceAlerts.com list upcoming events across various industries worldwide.

2. Professional Networks

- **National Speakers Association (NSA) and Global Speakers Federation (GSF)**: Being part of these types of organizations provides networking opportunities, professional development, and access to member-only resources.
- **Industry associations**: Join associations related to your field to connect with professionals who might need speakers for workshops, seminars, or webinars.
- **Chamber of Commerce**: Local and regional chambers often host events and are a good source for speaking opportunities in the business community.
- **Professional groups**: LinkedIn groups, Facebook groups, or local meetup groups can be excellent places to find leads and network with other professionals.

3. Direct Research

- **Conference calendars**: Regularly check calendars of major conferences in your sectors; these are often published well in advance.

- **Industry publications**: Keeping up with your industry's major publications can alert you to new opportunities and upcoming events.
- **Social media announcements**: Follow organizations and influencers in your field on platforms like X and LinkedIn to learn about new events and speaker calls.
- **Professional forums**: Participate in online forums where professionals discuss upcoming events and opportunities.

Building Relationships for Opportunities

1. Network Development

- **Attend industry events**: Whether virtual or in-person, attending events is crucial for making connections that may lead to speaking opportunities.
- **Join professional associations**: Active participation can make you a go-to expert when members need speakers.
- **Participate in speaker groups**: Groups specifically for speakers can provide tips on finding speaking opportunities and may offer direct leads.
- **Build relationships with event planners**: Establishing a rapport with event planners can lead to repeated bookings and referrals.

2. Leveraging Existing Connections

- **Partner with established speakers**: These speakers can provide introductions and recommend you for events where they cannot speak.
- **Get introductions to decision-makers**: Use your network to connect directly with those who decide on speakers for events.
- **Build referral networks**: Encourage past clients to refer you to others and consider offering incentives for successful referrals.
- **Maintain contact with past clients**: Regular updates and check-ins keep you on their radar for future events.

Conclusion

Finding speaking opportunities is a multi-faceted process that involves proactive lead generation, strategic relationship building, and effective utilization of existing networks. By employing a mix of these strategies, you can increase your visibility, establish your credibility, and expand your professional speaking career. Each speaking engagement is an opportunity to further build your reputation and open doors to more events, creating a cycle of success.

Evaluating Speaking Opportunities

When considering various speaking opportunities, it's essential to conduct a thorough evaluation to ensure that the event aligns with your professional goals and standards. This involves looking at the event's legitimacy, audience fit, professional development value, logistical considerations, and potential red flags.

Assessment Criteria

1. Event Legitimacy

- **Organization Reputation**: Research the hosting organization's background. Positive reviews, well-known industry presence, and endorsements from reputable entities are good indicators.
- **Event History**: Look for events with a successful track record. New events can also be promising if organized by credible groups.
- **Professional Website**: A well-maintained website with clear, professional content suggests a well-organized event.
- **Updated Contact Information**: Ensure that the contact details are current; this reflects the organizer's reliability and accessibility.

2. Audience Fit

- **Target Demographic Match**: The event should cater to an audience that aligns with your speaking topics and desired reach.
- **Industry Alignment**: The event should pertain to industries you are either experienced in or looking to enter.
- **Content Relevance**: Your expertise should directly address the interests or needs of the event's audience.
- **Experience Level Appropriateness**: Ensure the event's attendee experience level matches your content's complexity or simplicity.

3. Professional Development Value

- **Networking Opportunities**: Consider whether the event will allow you to connect with peers, industry leaders, or potential clients.
- **Industry Exposure**: Assess if speaking at the event will enhance your visibility and credibility within your industry.
- **Portfolio Building**: Determine if the engagement will add significant value to your portfolio and help attract future opportunities.
- **Testimonial Potential**: Identify opportunities for gathering testimonials, which can bolster your professional profile.

4. Logistical Considerations

- **Travel Requirements**: Consider the distance, cost, and time involved in traveling to the event.
- **Time Commitment**: Evaluate the duration of the event and your required involvement to ensure it fits within your schedule.
- **Technical Support**: Check the availability of necessary technical resources and support for your presentation.
- **Resource Needs**: Assess if additional resources (e.g., handouts, technical equipment) will be required and whether the event organizer will provide them.

Red Flags to Watch For

1. Outdated Information

- **Old Websites**: An outdated website may indicate a lack of organization or commitment.
- **Past Deadlines**: Information or applications with past deadlines that haven't been updated suggest poor management.
- **Inactive Social Media**: Lack of recent activity on social media platforms may suggest low engagement or poor event promotion.
- **Discontinued Events**: Ensure the event is still active and not listed from previous years without updates.

2. Communication Issues

- **Unclear Expectations**: Vague descriptions of your role or the audience can lead to ineffective presentations.
- **Delayed Responses**: Slow or no responses to inquiries can indicate disorganization.
- **Unprofessional Correspondence**: Poor communication, errors, and an unprofessional tone are major red flags.
- **Missing Contact Details**: Incomplete or missing contact information can be a sign of potential issues.

Conclusion

Careful evaluation of speaking opportunities can prevent potential professional pitfalls and ensure that each engagement contributes positively to your career growth. Use these criteria to make informed decisions that align with your professional objectives and enhance your professional speaking portfolio.

Maximizing Conference Attendance

Attending a conference is not just about showing up and giving a talk. To capitalize on the opportunity, it's essential to engage in strategic participation that extends before, during, and after the event. Here's how to maximize your conference attendance effectively:

Pre-Event Planning

1. **Research Attendees**: Before the event, find out who will be attending and identify key individuals with whom you want to connect. Look for potential clients, industry influencers, or fellow speakers with whom you can form strategic partnerships.
2. **Prepare Marketing Materials**: Have your business cards, brochures, or even a digital portfolio ready. If applicable, prepare a small giveaway that can help make your interactions memorable.
3. **Set Networking Goals**: Define what you aim to achieve at the conference. It could be as simple as making a certain number of new contacts, arranging follow-up meetings, or finding potential leads for future speaking engagements.
4. **Plan Follow-Up Strategy**: Organize how you will follow up with the contacts you make. This could involve scheduling emails, planning phone calls, or setting reminders to connect on social media.

On-Site Activities

1. **Attend Other Sessions**: Show your engagement and support for the event by attending other speakers' sessions. This can provide additional networking opportunities and help you gain

insights into current industry trends and topics.
2. **Meet Event Planners**: Introduce yourself to the event organizers and express your appreciation. Building a rapport with them can lead to more speaking invitations at future events.
3. **Network with Attendees**: Use breaks, lunches, and social gatherings to meet attendees. Be proactive but genuine in your interactions. Ask insightful questions and listen actively to understand how you might help them or collaborate in the future.
4. **Collect Contact Information**: Whenever possible, collect business cards or contact details. Make notes on the cards to remember key points from your conversation, which will be helpful during follow-up.

Post-Event Follow-Up

1. **Send Thank You Notes**: Send a personalized thank you message to the people you met. Mention specific details from your conversation to remind them of your interaction.
2. **Connect on Social Media**: Add your new contacts on LinkedIn, X, or other relevant social

media platforms. Engage with their content regularly to keep your connection active.
3. **Share Event Highlights**: Post about your experience at the conference on your social media and professional platforms. Tag the event, other speakers, or attendees to increase engagement.
4. **Maintain Relationships**: Continue to engage with your new contacts over time. Share relevant articles, send congratulatory notes on their achievements, or reach out with opportunities for collaboration. Regular contact keeps the relationship strong and keeps you on their radar for future opportunities.

Conclusion

By strategically planning your participation before, during, and after a conference, you not only enhance your experience but also increase your professional visibility and opportunities for growth. Each phase of the conference—from preparation to follow-up—plays a crucial role in maximizing your return on investment from attending the event.

Case Studies

Case Study 1: The Power of Being Present

Background: I was invited to present at the Southern Regional Business Conference. In addition to many of my peers, I viewed this as more than another speaking engagement but as a prime opportunity to forge valuable professional relationships.

Strategy: I chose to immerse myself fully in the conference experience, arriving a day early and planning to stay through the end.

Actions Taken:

1. **Early Arrival**: I arrived a day before the presentation, giving myself time to settle in and prepare for proactive engagement rather than just focusing on the speech.
2. **Engaging as a Peer**: At the opening reception and throughout the event, I introduced myself as a colleague interested in the industry rather than leading with my speaker status. This approach facilitated deeper, more genuine conversations.
3. **Building Rapport**: I strategically engaged in discussions about the challenges and goals of other attendees without immediately trying to steer the conversation towards my services.

This approach enabled me to learn about how I could help others.
4. **Active Participation**: I attended other sessions before my own, actively participating and integrating insights from those sessions into my presentation, thereby demonstrating my commitment to the event beyond my speaking role.
5. **Post-Presentation Engagement**: After my session, I continued to participate in the conference, attending workshops and the closing dinner, which provided additional networking opportunities.

Outcomes:

- **Enhanced Credibility**: By participating in various facets of the conference and integrating what I learned into the presentations, I enhanced my credibility as a committed industry participant.
- **Relationship Building**: My interactions led to a significant connection with an event coordinator for a large manufacturing association, who later introduced me to other key contacts.
- **Future Engagements**: I secured speaking engagements with two organizations within three months following the conference.
- **Long-term Professional Relationships**: The relationships I developed during the conference

continued to offer opportunities and collaborations for years, proving the long-term value of this strategy.

Lessons Learned:

- **Full Engagement**: I demonstrated that being fully engaged in a conference—beyond just the time spent on stage—can significantly amplify a speaker's impact and lead to substantial professional opportunities.
- **Peer-to-Peer Interaction**: Approaching other attendees as peers and showing genuine interest in their challenges can position a speaker as a relatable and approachable professional.
- **Strategic Networking**: Staying through the entire event and participating in less formal settings like meals and receptions can lead to informal interactions that may result in valuable business opportunities.

Conclusion:

My experience highlights the importance of viewing speaking engagements as more than just a platform for delivery. By fully engaging with the event and its participants, speakers can enhance their professional reputation, forge meaningful connections, and open doors to future opportunities. This case study serves as a compelling argument for the benefits of active and thoughtful participation in industry events, highlighting that true presence involves both physical and mental engagement.

Case Study 2: From Free to Fee - Margaret's Strategic Approach to Unpaid Speaking Engagements

Background: Margaret, an advocate for domestic violence awareness, faced a common dilemma for many emerging speakers: how to transition from unpaid to paid speaking opportunities. When presented with a free speaking slot at a local Chamber of Commerce breakfast, she saw potential where others saw a lack of value.

Strategy: Margaret decided to treat the unpaid speaking opportunity as an investment. Understanding the audience's composition—30 local business owners and community leaders—she tailored her presentation to highlight the impact of domestic violence on workplace productivity and safety, topics highly relevant to her audience.

Actions Taken:

1. **Customized Presentation:**
    - Margaret did not use a generic speech. Instead, she researched the businesses attending and customized her content to

resonate with their specific industries, focusing on actionable insights.
2. **Professional Preparation**:
    - She arrived early, dressed professionally, and brought well-prepared handouts that not only discussed domestic violence but also provided actionable steps for businesses to support affected employees. These handouts also featured her contact information and credentials prominently.
3. **Engaging Delivery**:
    - Her 20-minute presentation was solution-oriented, using a single compelling story and three actionable strategies rather than overwhelming the audience with statistics.
4. **Effective Follow-up**:
    - After the event, Margaret promptly followed up with personalized emails to those who had expressed interest, offering additional tailored resources. She also sent a thank-you note to the Chamber president, volunteering to contribute to their newsletter, which was accepted.
5. **Continuous Engagement**:
    - She connected with each attendee on LinkedIn and continued to share content that positioned her as a resource in both

domestic violence awareness and broader business leadership topics.

Outcomes:

- **Immediate Interest**: Several attendees approached Margaret post-presentation with questions, indicating engagement and interest.
- **Subsequent Opportunities**: Within two months, she received invitations to speak at three other Chamber events, this time with honoraria. A local manufacturing company hired her for sensitivity training, recognizing the value she could bring to their organization.
- **Keynote Engagement**: Positive feedback from her initial talk led to an invitation to deliver a keynote at the regional Chamber conference, a paid opportunity that also opened doors to further engagements across the state.
- **Financial Impact**: The unpaid 20-minute slot ultimately generated over $15,000 in speaking fees, validating her strategy of viewing unpaid opportunities as strategic investments.

Conclusion:

Margaret Hodges' experience highlights a strategic approach to unpaid speaking engagements. By delivering tailored, high-quality content and focusing on building relationships rather than making immediate sales, she effectively converted a free opportunity into a significant boost for her speaking career. This case study serves as a powerful example for speakers on how professionalism, strategic preparation, and proactive follow-up can turn seemingly low-value opportunities into pivotal career advancements.

Case Study 3: Conference Circuit Success - Rebecca's Entry into the Healthcare Industry

Background: Rebecca, an established speaker on leadership and resilience with a project management background, sought to pivot her expertise into the healthcare sector, despite lacking direct industry experience or credentials. Facing challenges in gaining traction through conventional proposal submissions, Rebecca shifted her strategy to immerse herself in the industry through direct engagement.

Strategy: Rebecca's approach centered on deep industry immersion, strategic networking, and leveraging serendipitous opportunities to demonstrate her expertise in a new context.

Actions Taken:

1. **Industry Immersion as an Attendee:**
   - Rebecca registered for the National Healthcare Management Conference, not as a speaker but as an attendee,

investing in learning the sector's language, challenges, and trends through firsthand experiences.
2. **Pre-Conference Preparation:**
    - Before the conference, she thoroughly researched the healthcare industry's current challenges and familiarized herself with specific terminology and trends to effectively communicate with healthcare professionals.
3. **Active Participation and Networking:**
    - At the conference, Rebecca engaged deeply with the content, participated actively in discussions, and used networking opportunities to connect with influential industry professionals, including the event's organizer.
4. **Seizing Opportunistic Offers:**
    - When a panelist slot opened unexpectedly, Rebecca tactfully demonstrated her relevant expertise pulling from her background in project management, which led to an invitation to join a panel discussion.
5. **Panel Participation and Follow-Up:**
    - During the panel, she skillfully connected her leadership insights to healthcare-specific challenges, contributing thoughtfully without overstepping her non-healthcare

background. Post-panel, she followed up with attendees and panel members, sharing customized resources and maintaining ongoing communication, particularly with the event coordinator.

Outcomes:

- **Immediate Recognition**: Rebecca's insightful contribution to the panel significantly raised her profile among the conference attendees and organizers.
- **Subsequent Opportunities**: Her successful panel appearance and proactive follow-up led to an invitation from the event organizer to speak at a regional healthcare conference, this time as a featured speaker paying her requested fee.
- **Further Engagements**: The regional conference appearance led to additional bookings at healthcare conferences, each opportunity utilized to refine her presentations to be more tailored to healthcare professionals.
- **Established Industry Presence**: Within 11 months, Rebecca successfully positioned herself as a credible speaker in healthcare leadership circles, respected for her expertise and her willingness to adapt and learn about the industry's specific challenges.

Conclusion:

Rebecca's strategic shift from traditional speaking engagements to immersive industry participation exemplifies how speakers can enter new sectors effectively. Her success emphasizes the importance of:

- **Preparation**: Understanding the industry's language and challenges to communicate effectively.
- **Networking**: Engaging with key individuals at conferences to showcase expertise and acquire new insights.
- **Flexibility**: Adapting one's expertise to the specific needs and contexts of the target audience.
- **Follow-up**: Building lasting relationships that convert into speaking opportunities.

Key Lesson: Rebecca's journey highlights that breaking into a new industry as a speaker is feasible with a strategic approach that combines humility, genuine interest, and a readiness to adapt one's expertise to meet industry-specific needs. This case study serves as a blueprint for speakers aiming to diversify their speaking career into new domains.

Case Study 4: Virtual Pivot Success - Camille's Transformation

Background: Camille, a professional speaker and life coach, known for her dynamic in-person presentations, faced a significant challenge when the pandemic shifted the landscape of on-site presentations to virtual platforms. With a major technology conference transitioning online, Camille had to quickly adapt her approach to maintain her speaking engagements and income.

Strategy: Camille's strategy involved a rapid acquisition of new technical skills and equipment, a reconfiguration of her presentation style to suit the virtual format, and proactive problem-solving with technical rehearsals.

Actions Taken:

1. **Equipment Upgrade:**
    - Recognizing the limitations of her existing hardware, Camille invested in a mid-range webcam, a ring light, and a simple microphone, enhancing her video and audio quality for virtual presentations.
2. **Home Studio Setup:**
    - She transformed a corner of her home office into a professional-looking studio, utilizing bookshelves and a professional

banner as a backdrop to convey a polished image.
3. **Presentation Redesign:**
    - Camille revised her presentation to fit the virtual format, focusing on shorter segments, more engaging visuals, and interactive elements such as polls and chat functionalities to compensate for the lack of physical presence.
4. **Technical Proficiency and Rehearsal:**
    - She familiarized herself with the virtual platform and rehearsed, which helped identify and rectify issues with slide compatibility and video lagging ahead of the actual event.
5. **Live Presentation Execution:**
    - During the conference, Camille effectively engaged the virtual audience with a mix of polls, chat interactions, and direct questioning, maintaining a high energy level and smooth management of technical elements.

Outcomes:

- **Positive Feedback and Recognition:**
    - The success of her presentation not only secured Camille's position as a capable virtual presenter but also led the conference organizer to request that she

write a guide for other speakers struggling with the virtual format.
- **Establishing Expertise in a New Niche**:
  - Camille's guide on virtual presentations was distributed by the conference to its speakers, establishing her as an expert in virtual presenting and leading to new opportunities for virtual presentation coaching.
- **Creation of New Revenue Streams**:
  - Within seven months, Camille developed a lucrative coaching service for other speakers needing to adapt to virtual presentations, significantly expanding her business beyond traditional speaking.
- **Expansion Beyond Geographical Boundaries**:
  - The shift to virtual events allowed Camille to reach a global audience, leading to more frequent speaking engagements and higher fees due to her now proven capability to deliver compelling virtual presentations.

Conclusion:

Camille's swift pivot from in-person to virtual presentations exemplifies resilience and adaptability in the face of industry disruptions. Her ability to quickly learn and implement new technologies, redesign her presentation style, and proactively solve potential technical issues played a crucial role in her continued success during the pandemic. This case study highlights the importance of flexibility and the willingness to embrace new challenges as opportunities for growth and expansion, proving that even in crisis, proactive and innovative actions can lead to substantial professional advancements and new business avenues.

Practical Exercises: Opportunity Analysis Workshop

This exercise is designed to help you systematically evaluate speaking opportunities using a structured approach. By assessing each event's potential benefits against its demands, you can make informed decisions that align with your career goals and resources.

Exercise 1: Opportunity Analysis Workshop

Part A: Create Your Evaluation System

1. **Set Up a Comprehensive Spreadsheet**:
   - Columns to Include:
     - Event Name and Organization
     - Date and Location
     - Target Audience

- Application Requirements
- Deadline
- Potential Value (Rate from 1 to 5)
- Follow-up Status
- Travel Costs
- Speaking Fee
- Decision Maker Contact Info
- Notes/Special Requirements

2. **Instructions**:
   - Use a spreadsheet tool like Microsoft Excel or Google Sheets.
   - Input sample data for each column to understand how the system works.
   - Adjust the columns as necessary to fit specific needs or insights you wish to track.

Part B: Opportunity Evaluation Practice

Sample Speaking Opportunities:

1. **Local Chamber Monthly Meeting**:
   - **Details**: Unpaid, 20 minutes, 50 local business owners, Thursday morning, 5 miles away.
   - **Evaluation Criteria**:
     - **Financial Value**: (0/5) — ability to generate revenue
     - **Network Potential**: (3/5) — potential local business connections

- **Brand Building:** (3/5) — good for local visibility
- **Future Opportunities:** (3/5) — could lead to paid local engagements
- **Resource Requirements:** (5/5) — minimal travel and preparation needed

2. **Regional Industry Conference:**
   - **Details:** $2,500 fee, 45-minute keynote, 300 attendees, requires travel, highly visible event.
   - **Evaluation Criteria:**
     - **Financial Value:** (5/5) — ability to generate revenue
     - **Network Potential:** (5/5) — exposure to a larger to national audience
     - **Brand Building:** (5/5) — significant visibility in the industry
     - **Future Opportunities:** (4/5) — potential for industry-specific engagements
     - **Resource Requirements:** (3/5) — involves travel and extensive preparation

3. **Virtual Training Session:**
   - **Details:** $1,000 fee, 2-hour workshop, 25 participants, no travel, potential for repeat business.
   - **Evaluation Criteria:**
     - **Financial Value:** (3/5) — ability to generate revenue
     - **Network Potential:** (2/5) — limited interaction in a virtual setting
     - **Brand Building:** (3/5) — niche audience development
     - **Future Opportunities:** (4/5) — strong potential for recurring workshops
     - **Resource Requirements:** (5/5) — minimal logistical demands

Instructions for Completing Part B:

- Use the criteria and details provided to evaluate each speaking opportunity.
- Rate each opportunity based on the provided criteria using a scale of 1 to 5, with 5 being the highest.
- Summarize the scores to determine which opportunity aligns best with your strategic goals.

By conducting these exercises, you can develop a robust framework for evaluating speaking opportunities. This systematic approach ensures you consider all critical factors, helping you prioritize engagements that offer the greatest benefits relative to their costs and demands.

Exercise 2: Network Mapping Deep Dive

This exercise helps you systematically evaluate and optimize your professional network for increased visibility and new opportunities in your speaking career. By mapping your network and planning strategic interactions, you can effectively leverage your connections.

Step 1: Connection Inventory

Instructions: Create four lists in a spreadsheet or a dedicated CRM tool to categorize and detail your connections.

1. **Direct Professional Contacts**
    - **Current Clients**: List all active clients with whom you have ongoing projects.
    - **Past Clients**: Include clients with whom you've worked previously but do not have current engagements.
    - **Colleagues**: Note colleagues from current and previous workplaces, collaborations, or projects.
    - **Industry Peers**: Include professionals you've met at conferences, seminars, or

through mutual connections but aren't currently working with directly.

2. **Organization Affiliations**
    - **Professional Associations**: Memberships in organizations related to your field of expertise
    - **Alumni Groups**: Connections from educational institutions attended
    - **Volunteer Organizations**: Contacts from charitable or community service involvement
    - **Social Groups**: Connections from non-professional but potentially useful networks (e.g., clubs or local groups)

3. **Online Networks**
    - **LinkedIn Connections**: Professional connections specific to your LinkedIn network
    - **Facebook Groups**: Membership in professional and industry-specific groups
    - **Professional Forums**: Participation in online forums related to your field
    - **Industry Platforms**: Engagement on specialized platforms that cater to your industry or speaking topics

4. **Media Contacts**
    - **Journalists**: Contacts who report in your field's industry or general interest areas
    - **Bloggers**: Influencers who might share interests in your topics or industry
    - **Podcasters**: Hosts who discuss topics relevant to your expertise
    - **Publishers**: Editors and publishers who work within your industry's trade publications

Step 2: Opportunity Analysis

Instructions: Evaluate each connection category to identify key opportunities and plan your approach.

1. **Identify Decision Makers**: In each category, pinpoint individuals who have the authority to invite you to speak, collaborate, or promote your work.
2. **Note Upcoming Events**: Track any events these connections are involved with, which could be potential platforms for your speaking engagements.
3. **List Potential Introductions**: Identify whom among your connections can introduce you to new decision-makers or influencers.
4. **Rate Relationship Strength (1-5)**: Assess the strength of each relationship, based on past interactions, mutual benefits, and response rates.

Step 3: Action Plan Development

Instructions: Define specific, actionable strategies to enhance and utilize your network effectively.

1. **Monthly Contact Goals**: Set targets for how often you will reach out to each category of your network, such as sending a monthly newsletter, industry updates, or checking in.
2. **Content Sharing Strategy**: Plan how you will share relevant content with different segments of your network. This might include writing articles for LinkedIn, sharing research with professional groups, or posting insights on industry forums.
3. **Meeting Schedules**: Schedule regular meetings or calls with key individuals, particularly those who can provide opportunities.
4. **Collaboration Opportunities**: Identify potential partnership projects, such as joint webinars, co-authored papers, or panel discussions at industry events.

By following these steps, you can create a robust strategy for leveraging your professional network, enhancing your visibility in your industry, and uncovering new opportunities for speaking engagements and joint-efforts. This organized approach ensures that you maintain and grow your network in a way that supports your professional goals.

Exercise 3: Annual Planning Workshop

This exercise is designed to help speakers strategically plan their year to maximize opportunities and reach their professional goals. Through careful planning and goal setting, you can ensure a balanced approach to securing speaking engagements, enhancing relationships, and developing your expertise.

Part A: Calendar Development

Instructions: Develop a multi-layered calendar to track and plan all relevant activities and deadlines throughout the year.

1. **Annual Overview:**
    - **Major Industry Conferences**: List all important conferences in your field, including national and international engagements where you might want to speak or attend.
    - **Regional Events**: Include smaller, local events that can provide speaking opportunities and networking.
    - **Application Deadlines**: Mark deadlines for submitting speaking proposals to conferences and events.
    - **Professional Development**: Schedule times for training, workshops, or courses to enhance your skills.

2. **Quarterly Focus:**
   - **Speaking Engagements**: Plan which quarters you will focus on delivering presentations, considering seasonality and industry trends.
   - **Networking Events**: Identify key networking opportunities for each quarter to ensure consistent community engagement and visibility.
   - **Content Creation**: Allocate specific quarters for heavy content production, such as writing articles, creating presentation materials, or updating your website.
   - **Follow-up Activities**: Set aside time after events and engagements for follow-up actions to maximize the impact of your efforts.
3. **Monthly Action Items:**
   - **Outreach Targets**: List potential clients or event organizers you will contact each month.
   - **Proposal Deadlines**: Keep track of proposal submission deadlines for upcoming speaking opportunities.
   - **Preparation Time**: Allocate adequate time for preparing speeches, presentations, and travel logistics.
   - **Travel Arrangements**: Plan and book travel needs in advance to avoid

last-minute expenses and ensure a smooth itinerary.

Part B: Goal Setting

Instructions: Set clear, measurable goals for the year to guide your activities and track progress.

1. **Number of Speaking Engagements**: Decide how many speaking engagements you aim to secure monthly or annually.
2. **Revenue Goals**: Set specific financial targets from speaking fees, workshops, and any other related activities.
3. **New Network Connections**: Determine the number of new professional contacts you aim to make.
4. **Content Creation Schedule**: Outline a timeline for producing new content pieces, such as blog posts, articles, publications, videos, or podcasts.

Part C: Strategy Development

Instructions: Develop detailed strategies for each key area of your professional activities.

1. **Lead Generation:**
    - Utilize both online and offline methods to generate leads for potential speaking engagements, such as through industry

newsletters, speaker bureaus, and networking events.
2. **Relationship Building**:
   - Plan regular touchpoints with existing contacts and new leads through email updates, coffee meetings, or at industry events.
   - Cultivate relationships with event organizers and decision-makers in organizations relevant to your speaking topics.
3. **Content Development**:
   - Schedule regular periods for content creation, focusing on topics that align with your speaking niche.
   - Consider diversifying your content formats to include not only written articles but also videos, webinars, and interactive online content.
4. **Professional Development**:
   - Identify skills and knowledge areas for improvement and seek out specific training programs, courses, or conferences that can enhance your professional capabilities.
   - Set aside a budget for professional development to ensure you can take advantage of opportunities as they arise.

By meticulously planning each component of your professional activities, you can ensure a well-rounded approach to building a successful speaking career. This structured planning method not only helps in managing current opportunities but also in strategically positioning yourself for future growth.

Exercise 4: Speaking Opportunity Creation

This exercise is designed to help speakers proactively generate their own speaking opportunities by identifying market gaps, creating compelling event proposals, and forging strategic partnerships.

Identify Gaps

Instructions: Conduct a detailed analysis to identify areas where you can offer unique value.

1. **List Underserved Markets**:
   - Identify demographic groups or industry sectors that are currently underserved in your field. This could include emerging markets that have not been fully explored.
2. **Note Emerging Topics**:
   - Keep track of new developments, technologies, or challenges within your industry that have not been extensively covered in speaking circuits.
3. **Spot Industry Trends**:
   - Stay updated on the broader trends affecting your industry which could lead

to new speaking topics or areas of interest.
   4. **Find Unique Angles**:
      - Consider your personal expertise and experiences that offer a unique perspective on common issues or topics within your industry.

Develop Proposals

Instructions: Use the gaps identified to create innovative speaking event proposals.

   1. **Create Event Concepts**:
      - Develop concepts for events or conferences that could address the needs of underserved markets or topics.
   2. **Design Workshop Formats**:
      - Outline formats for workshops or seminars that focus on teaching skills or knowledge related to emerging topics.
   3. **Structure Series Ideas**:
      - Consider a series of talks or webinars that could provide ongoing value to your target audience.
   4. **Plan Virtual Options**:
      - Ensure that all your event ideas include virtual alternatives, considering the global shift towards digital platforms.

Build Partnership Plans

Instructions: Identify and propose collaborations with organizations or individuals who can help you bring your speaking events to life.

1. **Identify Potential Hosts**:
    - Look for organizations, educational institutions, or companies that align with your speaking topics and could host your event.
2. **Draft Collaboration Proposals**:
    - Prepare detailed proposals outlining how a partnership could benefit both parties, emphasizing the value and impact of your proposed events.
3. **Create Value Propositions**:
    - Define what makes your event unique and valuable to potential hosts and sponsors.
4. **Design Revenue Sharing Models**:
    - Propose financial models that make the partnership beneficial economically to all involved parties.

Key Takeaways

- **Quality Leads**: Focus on generating high-quality leads through thorough research and relationship-building.

- **Professional Presence**: Maintain a professional demeanor in all interactions to enhance credibility and reliability.
- **Consistent Follow-up**: Regularly engage with your contacts to keep your proposals top of mind and maintain professional relationships.

Action Items

1. **Subscribe to Lead Generation Services**:
   - Invest in services that can provide you with updated and relevant leads for speaking opportunities.
2. **Join Relevant Professional Associations**:
   - Gain access to networks and resources that can open doors to new speaking opportunities.
3. **Create an Opportunity Tracking System**:
   - Implement a system to keep track of all potential and in-progress speaking opportunities.
4. **Develop a Networking Strategy**:
   - Outline how you will approach networking events and what goals you aim to achieve from each interaction.
5. **Build a Calendar of Industry Events**:
   - Keep a calendar of major industry engagements and professional development opportunities that you can attend or target for speaking opportunities.

Remember, creating your own speaking opportunities involves not just identifying gaps and crafting proposals, but also actively building and nurturing professional relationships that can lead to successful events.

Chapter 5: The Application Process

Navigating the application process effectively is crucial for a professional speaker's success. This chapter provides a comprehensive guide to preparing and managing speaking applications with the level of professionalism that event planners and conference organizers expect.

Essential Application Materials

1. Professional Headshot

- **Requirements**:
    - High resolution (300 DPI minimum)
    - Professional attire
    - Neutral background

- Recent (within the last 2 years)
            - Available in both horizontal and vertical formats
            - Provided in multiple sizes for different uses
    - **Usage Guidelines**:
        - Website submissions
        - Marketing materials
        - Conference programs
        - Social media profiles
        - Press releases

2. Speaking Videos

- **Types Needed**:
    - Full unedited excerpt (up to 15 minutes)
    - Keynote excerpts (3-5 minutes)
    - Interactive workshop segments
    - Client testimonials
    - Behind-the-scenes preparation
    - Audience engagement moments
- **Technical Requirements**:
    - Professional quality audio
    - Multiple camera angles
    - Clear audience visibility
    - Proper lighting
    - Professional editing

3. Topic Submissions

- **Required Elements**:

- Primary topic title
- Secondary/alternate titles
- Topic categories
- Target audience description
- Industry relevance
- Customization options

4. Application Management System

- **Digital Organization:**
  - **Standard Materials Folder:** Keep a digital folder that includes headshots, bios, videos, topic descriptions, client testimonials, and marketing materials for easy access and submission.
- **Application Tracking System:**
  - Track event details, submission dates, follow-up schedules, contact information, status updates, and response tracking to manage multiple applications efficiently.
- **Login Management:**
  - Create consistent usernames and use a standardized password system for all application portals.
  - Maintain secure storage of credentials and document access details for each application portal.
  - Track registration requirements and deadlines for each event.

Best Practices for Application Success

1. **Tailor Applications**: Customize your application materials to reflect the specific themes and goals of each conference or event. This shows organizers that you have a deep understanding of their audience and event objectives.
2. **Follow Submission Guidelines**: Adhere strictly to the application instructions provided by event organizers. This includes deadlines, formats, and any specific questions or requirements they have listed.
3. **Quality Control**: Before submitting any materials, ensure they are polished and free of errors. This includes reviewing video quality, proofreading all written materials, and confirming that photos and videos are updated.
4. **Leverage Technology**: Utilize CRM systems to manage your applications and keep track of all interactions with event organizers. This can help streamline the process and ensure you don't miss any opportunities or follow-up actions.
5. **Network and Follow-Up**: After submitting an application, use your network to find connections who can advocate on your behalf. Additionally, a polite follow-up email or call can help keep your application top of mind for organizers.

By following these guidelines and using the tools suggested, you can enhance your visibility in the speaker selection process and increase your chances of being selected for high-profile speaking engagements.

The Application Process: A Detailed Guide for Professional Speakers

Navigating the application process for speaking opportunities can be daunting. Here is a structured approach to help you manage this process effectively, broken down into three key phases: Pre-Application, Submission, and Follow-Up.

1. Pre-Application Phase

The groundwork laid before you even fill out an application form is crucial. Proper preparation can significantly increase your chances of success.

- **Research The Organization**: Begin by understanding the event or conference's theme, its audience, and the organization's mission. This information will guide your application and help tailor your materials to their needs.
- **Verify Submission Deadlines**: Note all relevant deadlines to ensure you don't miss any opportunities. Consider setting reminders a few days before the deadline as a precaution.

- **Review Past Speakers**: Analyzing the profiles of past speakers can give insights into the event's preferences and standards. This can help you position yourself similarly or find a unique angle that stands out.
- **Check Technical Requirements**: For virtual events or specific venues, understanding the technical setup and requirements is essential to ensure your presentation can be delivered smoothly.
- **Prepare Customized Materials**: Tailor your proposal, bio, headshots, and speaking videos to align closely with the event's focus and expected audience. Customization can make a significant difference in showing event organizers that you are a suitable match.

2. Submission Phase

Filling out and submitting your application is more than just a bureaucratic step; it's your first impression.

- **Complete All Required Fields**: Ensure that no part of the application is left incomplete. Incomplete applications are often the first to be discarded.
- **Provide Supplementary Materials**: Include additional materials like videos, publications, or testimonials that can enhance your application and showcase your expertise and experience.

- **Double-Check Attachments**: Before sending, make sure all attachments open correctly and are the correct files. This helps avoid the common pitfall of submitting corrupt or wrong files.
- **Verify Submission Receipt**: After submitting, ensure you receive a confirmation email or notification. If not, follow up to confirm receipt.
- **Save Confirmation Details**: Keep a record of all submission confirmations and reference numbers for future correspondence or follow-up.

3. Follow-Up Phase

The process doesn't end with the submission; active follow-up can keep your application top of mind for organizers.

- **Track Application Status**: Use a system to regularly check and update the status of each application. This can be a spreadsheet or a more sophisticated CRM tool.
- **Send Professional Follow-Ups**: Approximately 10 days after submission, a polite follow-up email can demonstrate your enthusiasm and professionalism. It can also ensure that your application hasn't been overlooked.
- **Document All Communication**: Keep records of all interactions with the event organizers. This

includes dates, the content of communication, and any feedback or comments they provide.
- **Maintain Contact Records**: Update your contact list with details from the application process, which can be invaluable for future applications or networking opportunities.
- **Update Tracking System**: Regularly update your tracking system with the latest information from interactions to stay organized and proactive.

By methodically approaching each phase of the application process, you enhance your visibility and viability as a candidate for speaking engagements. This structured approach not only organizes your efforts but also maximizes your opportunities to secure desired speaking slots.

Professional Communication Strategies

Effective communication is essential for professional speakers navigating the application process and maintaining relationships in the industry. Here are strategic approaches to ensure your communications are professional and impactful at every stage.

1. Initial Contact

Your first communication sets the tone for your professional relationship. Here's how to make sure it's impactful:

- **Professional Email Format**: Use a standard business format for your emails. This includes a polite greeting, a body structured for clarity, and a formal closing.
- **Clear Subject Lines**: Your subject line should be direct and informative. For example, "Proposal Submission: [Your Topic/Your Name]" clearly indicates the purpose of the email.
- **Concise Message Content**: Keep your email body concise. Make sure every sentence has a purpose. Clearly state your intentions, requests, or responses without unnecessary detail.
- **Relevant Attachments**: Include only necessary attachments. Ensure they are properly formatted and named so the recipient knows what they are before opening them.
- **Professional Signature**: End with a professional signature that includes your full name, title, and contact information, as well as links to your professional website or LinkedIn profile.

2. Follow-Up Protocol

Follow-up communication is crucial for maintaining engagement and showing your interest and professionalism.

- **Timing Guidelines**: Follow up within a week after your initial contact or a week after submitting an application or proposal. This shows interest without being too aggressive.
- **Response Templates**: Prepare templates for common responses to save time and maintain consistency. Customize them for each interaction to keep the message personal.
- **Status Inquiry Format**: When inquiring about the status of an application or proposal, be polite and express your continued interest. Example: *"I hope this message finds you well. I am writing to inquire about the status of my application for [Event/Position], submitted on [Date]. I am very enthusiastic about the opportunity to contribute."*
- **Thank You Messages**: Always send a thank you message after interviews, meetings, or after receiving helpful information. In addition to showing professionalism it also helps build and maintain relationships.
- **Networking Opportunities**: Use follow-up interactions as a chance to suggest further communication, such as a brief meeting or

phone call, to discuss potential collaborative opportunities or gain insights.

3. Application Status Management

Keeping track of your applications and communications are essential for managing numerous opportunities effectively.

- **Confirmation Tracking**: Always ensure you receive a confirmation after submitting applications. If not, follow up to confirm receipt.
- **Response Documentation**: Keep a record of all responses you receive. Note dates, key information provided, and any feedback or decisions.
- **Timeline Monitoring**: Monitor and record the timelines communicated by your contacts for decisions or next steps. This helps you follow up appropriately and keeps you prepared for upcoming tasks.
- **Decision Tracking**: Track decisions on applications or proposals, including acceptances, rejections, or requests for more information. This helps you understand trends and areas for improvement in your proposals.
- **Future Opportunity Notes**: Maintain notes on potential future opportunities mentioned by

contacts during interactions. This information is valuable for long-term planning and relationship building.

Implementing these strategies will help ensure that your professional communication is effective, timely, and conducive to building strong professional relationships. These practices not only facilitate success in securing speaking opportunities but also aid in establishing a respected presence within your professional community.

Bonus Application Elements

To enhance your speaking applications and make them stand out, incorporating detailed and compelling elements can significantly boost your attractiveness to event organizers. Here are some key bonus elements you can include in your applications to showcase your unique offerings and dedication:

1. Interaction Statements

Interaction statements demonstrate how you engage with your audience, making your presentations more appealing by highlighting active participation rather than passive listening.

- **Sample Interaction Statement:**
    - *"My presentations are dynamic and interactive, featuring proven engagement techniques such as real-time polling, small group discussions, case study analysis, and interactive exercises. Each session is designed to maintain high energy and ensure active participation, making the learning experience both educational and enjoyable."*

2. Value Propositions

A strong value proposition clearly outlines the benefits participants will gain from attending your session. It connects your presentation directly to the needs of the audience and the objectives of the event.

- **Sample Value Proposition:**
    - *"Participants leave my sessions equipped with practical tools that can be implemented immediately, customized resources tailored to address their specific challenges, and access to ongoing support through my extensive professional network. This ensures immediate learning and sustained application and improvement."*

3. Customization Statements

Customization statements address your willingness and ability to tailor your presentations to the specific needs of the audience and the organization, showing that you are attentive and adaptable.

- **Sample Customization Statement**:
    - "I ensure each presentation is meticulously tailored to meet your organization's specific needs. This customization process includes thorough pre-event research, interviews with key stakeholders, and the development of custom case studies that are directly relevant to your industry. This approach guarantees that the content is not only relevant but also directly applicable."

How to Incorporate These Elements in Your Application

- **Integrate into Proposals**: When submitting proposals, incorporate these statements to articulate the unique benefits and tailored approaches of your presentations.
- **Highlight in Marketing Materials**: Use these statements in your marketing materials, such as brochures or websites, to communicate the value and customization you bring to your speaking engagements.

- **Discuss in Pre-Event Meetings**: When meeting with event organizers, highlight these aspects of your presentation style to set yourself apart from other speakers.
- **Feature in Follow-Up Communications**: Include these elements in your follow-up communication with potential clients to reinforce the unique aspects of your offerings.

By adding these bonus elements to your applications and promotional efforts, you can significantly enhance the perception of your speaking services, making your proposals more compelling and increasing your chances of being selected for prestigious speaking opportunities.

Case Studies

Case Study 1: The Thorough Applicant - Crafting a Winning Application for the National Healthcare Conference

This case study examines how a speaker's calculated approach to the application process for a national healthcare conference resulted in their selection as a keynote speaker. By going beyond the basic requirements and providing detailed, relevant supplemental materials, the speaker demonstrated a deep understanding of the industry and the needs of the conference.

Background

The National Healthcare Leadership Summit issued a call for speakers, specifying required and optional application materials. The conference sought presenters who could contribute meaningful insights and innovations in healthcare management.

Scenario

Upon receiving the initial call for applications, the speaker was asked to provide a bio, headshot, and a topic description. Optional materials included evidence of previous healthcare speaking engagements, relevant industry certifications, and strategies for engaging the audience.

Speaker's Response

- **Required Materials**: The speaker submitted a professional bio that highlighted their expertise in healthcare communication, a high-resolution headshot, and a compelling topic description focusing on innovative communication strategies in healthcare settings.

- **Optional Materials:**
    - **Video Clips**: Submitted clips from a recent workshop on hospital management, demonstrating their dynamic speaking style and relevant content.
    - **Case Studies**: Included detailed case studies from three healthcare organizations that had implemented the speaker's communication strategies, showing tangible improvements in operations.
    - **Statistics**: Provided statistics evidencing a 27% improvement in patient satisfaction following their programs, showcasing the impact of their work.
    - **Testimonials**: Attached testimonials from directors at two leading medical centers, affirming the speaker's contributions to enhancing healthcare communication.
    - **Audience Engagement Plan**: Outlined a detailed plan for engaging the audience through interactive medical scenarios, ensuring the session would be participatory and directly applicable.

Result

The speaker was selected as the keynote speaker for the conference.

Follow-up Comment from the Selection Committee

The selection committee noted, *"Your thorough application demonstrated a deep understanding of our industry. The additional materials showed initiative and professionalism."*

Analysis

1. **Understanding the Audience**: The speaker clearly understood the conference's focus on healthcare leadership and tailored their application to meet these specific interests.
2. **Going Beyond the Basics**: By submitting well-chosen optional materials, the speaker fulfilled the basic application requirements and also showcased their unique qualifications. In addition, the direct relevance of their work to the conference themes was also recognized.
3. **Evidence of Impact**: The inclusion of quantifiable improvements and high-profile testimonials provided credible evidence of the speaker's impact, persuading the committee of their capability to deliver valuable insights.
4. **Engagement Strategy**: The detailed plan for audience interaction addressed how the speaker would make the session insightful and engaging, an important aspect for conference

organizers who aim to provide practical value to attendees.

Conclusion

This case study exemplifies how thoroughly addressing both required and optional elements in a speaker application can significantly enhance a candidate's appeal. By strategically selecting additional materials that underscored their expertise and alignment with the conference's goals, the speaker effectively communicated their potential to contribute a standout session. This approach can serve as a model for other professionals aiming to secure prominent speaking opportunities in their respective fields.

Case Study 2: The Follow-Up Master - Securing a Corporate Training Series

This case study illustrates the strategic use of follow-up communication to secure a corporate training series. The speaker's systematic approach not only kept their application top of mind but also demonstrated their ongoing engagement and value alignment with the potential client's goals.

Background

The speaker applied to lead a corporate training series focused on leadership development for emerging leaders within a large organization.

Scenario and Communication Strategy

- Week 1 - Initial Application:
    - **Content**: The speaker submitted a detailed proposal for their "Leadership and Legacy" program, tailored specifically to the organization's needs.
    - **Tactics**: Highlighted customization of the content to reflect the organization's focus on nurturing emerging leaders.
- Week 2 - Value-Added Follow-up:
    - **Content**: Sent an article on developing millennial leaders that supports the themes of the proposed training program.
    - **Tactics**: Included annotations on three strategies within the article that complement and enrich the proposed workshop content, thereby enhancing the perceived value of their offering.
- Week 3 - Professional Check-in:
    - **Content**: A respectful follow-up inquiring about the application status, reiterating enthusiasm for the opportunity, and offering to provide

          further details or adapt the proposal as needed.
        - **Tactics**: Maintained professional decorum while ensuring the application remained active in the selection committee's considerations.
  - **Week 4 - Relationship Building**:
    - **Content**: Engaged with the potential client on LinkedIn, commenting on a post related to building inclusive leadership teams and sharing relevant research.
    - **Tactics**: Demonstrated ongoing engagement with the client's public content and aligned their own expertise with the client's expressed interests.

Result

The speaker was booked to lead the annual leadership development series and was later asked to develop additional programs for the organization.

Analysis

1. **Customized and Timely Follow-Ups**: Each follow-up added value or relevance to the initial proposal, showing the speaker's commitment and alignment with the organization's goals.
2. **Balanced Communication Frequency**: The speaker managed to keep the communication

frequent enough to stay on the radar without overwhelming the recipient, respecting the organization's timeline and processes.
3. **Strategic Content Sharing**: By sharing pertinent articles and personal research, the speaker reinforced their expertise and ongoing commitment to topics important to the potential client.
4. **Engagement Beyond Business**: Interacting on platforms like LinkedIn on topics relevant to the client's interests helped humanize the speaker and build a relationship beyond the transactional nature of the application process.

Conclusion

This case study serves as an excellent model for using follow-ups strategically to enhance the likelihood of success in competitive application processes. The speaker's approach shows that thoughtful, well-timed, and value-added communication can effectively differentiate a candidate. This demonstrates their expertise and also their proactive engagement and alignment with a potential client's broader goals. This methodical approach to follow-ups can be particularly effective in industries where building ongoing relationships is key to securing and expanding business opportunities.

Case Study 3: The Recovery Specialist - Navigating Technical Issues During Application Submission

This case study showcases how a speaker effectively handled a technical glitch during the application process, turning a potential setback into an opportunity to demonstrate professionalism and problem-solving skills.

Background

The speaker was in the process of submitting an application for a significant conference when they encountered technical issues with the online submission portal.

Scenario and Communication Strategy

- **Initial Problem:**
    - **Issue**: While attempting to submit the application through the conference's online portal, the system crashed, preventing the completion of the submission.
    - **Action Taken**: The speaker took screenshots of the error messages as evidence of the issue.
- **Speaker's Email Response:**
    - **Content**: The speaker promptly contacted the conference team via email,

explaining the situation clearly and providing screenshots to document the technical difficulties encountered.
    - **Options Proposed**:
        1. **Retry the online submission**: Asking if they should attempt to submit again once the issue is resolved.
        2. **Send materials via email**: Offering to send the application materials directly via email to bypass the problematic portal.
        3. **Schedule a call**: Proposing a discussion to explore alternative submission methods.
    - **Tone and Approach**: The email was composed with a professional tone, focusing on solving the issue efficiently while expressing a strong interest in participating in the conference.

Resolution

- **Organizer's Response**: The conference organizer appreciated the speaker's professional handling of the situation and provided a direct email address to submit the application materials, bypassing the faulty online portal.

- **Outcome**: The speaker successfully submitted their application via email, ensuring that their materials were received intact and on time.

Analysis

1. **Proactive Communication**: The speaker did not wait for the problem to escalate or for the organizers to notice a missed submission. They took immediate action to communicate the issue, which helped prevent misunderstandings or missed opportunities.
2. **Documentation**: By providing screenshots of the error, the speaker added credibility to their claim, making it easier for the organizers to understand the issue and justify the alternative submission method.
3. **Offering Solutions**: The speaker didn't just present a problem to the organizers; they also proposed multiple solutions, making it easier for the organizers to resolve the issue quickly and effectively.
4. **Maintaining Interest and Professionalism**: The speaker's clear interest in the conference and their professional handling of the situation likely contributed to a positive impression, enhancing their chances of being selected despite the technical difficulties.

Conclusion

This case study demonstrates the importance of swift and effective communication in the face of technical issues during application processes. By handling the situation professionally and offering practical solutions, the speaker was able to salvage the submission and maintain a positive relationship with the conference organizers. This proactive approach not only resolved the immediate issue but also showcased the speaker's problem-solving abilities and professionalism, qualities that are highly valued in any professional context.

Case Study 4: The Customization Expert - Tailoring Applications for Industry-Specific Needs

This case study illustrates how a speaker's ability to customize their presentation topic for a specific industry audience resulted in selection over more experienced competitors, emphasizing the value of audience-centric content in the application process.

Background

The speaker was preparing an application for a speaking slot at an industry-specific conference for IT professionals. The original topic, *"Communication with*

Less Confrontation," was broad and applicable to many fields.

Scenario and Customization Strategy

- **Original Topic**: *"Communication with Less Confrontation"*
    - A general topic focused on improving communication skills and reducing conflict in professional settings.
- **Customized Application**: *"Communication with Less Confrontation for IT Professionals"*
    - Recognizing the specific needs and challenges faced by IT professionals, especially in communicating complex technical information to non-technical stakeholders, the speaker tailored the application to address these unique challenges directly.
- **Customization Elements**:
    - **Real Coding Examples**: Used to illustrate key communication principles, making the content relatable and directly applicable for IT professionals.
    - **Tech-Specific Scenarios and Solutions**: Integrated scenarios that IT professionals might encounter, such as explaining software bugs to sales teams or discussing system requirements with clients.

- **Frameworks for Translating Technical Concepts**: Offered methods and frameworks to help IT staff effectively translate and communicate technical content to non-technical audiences.
- **Practical Exercises Using Actual Project Situations**: Designed to allow participants to practice new skills in contexts that mirror their everyday work environments, enhancing the learning experience and application of skills.

Result

The speaker was selected to present at the conference, chosen over other speakers who had more direct industry experience. The selection committee highlighted the application's tailored approach and the speaker's demonstrated understanding of the IT audience's specific communication challenges as key factors in their decision.

Analysis

1. **Audience-Centric Approach**: The speaker's decision to customize their presentation for the specific context of IT professionals demonstrated a deep understanding of the audience, directly addressing their unique challenges and needs.

2. **Relevance and Practicality**: By incorporating real-world coding examples and specific scenarios relevant to the attendees' daily tasks, the speaker ensured that the content was not only interesting but also practically useful.
3. **Engagement and Interaction**: The inclusion of practical exercises based on actual project situations suggested that the session would be interactive and hands-on. This is often more appealing to technical professionals who value practical, applicable knowledge.
4. **Competitive Advantage**: The detailed customization gave the speaker a competitive edge by showing a proactive effort to make the session valuable and relevant, surpassing even more experienced speakers in terms of perceived value and relevance.

Conclusion

This case study showcases the importance of tailoring speaking topics to the specific needs and contexts of the target audience, especially in industry-specific settings. Customization can significantly enhance the appeal of a proposal, demonstrating the speaker's commitment to providing value and addressing the unique challenges of the audience. By focusing on the specific needs of IT professionals and providing actionable, relevant solutions, the speaker was able to stand out in the application process and secure a coveted speaking opportunity.

Application Templates

1. Initial Application Email Template - Detailed Guide

When you're applying to speak at a conference, your initial application email is crucial. It needs to convey all the necessary information and also capture the attention of the conference organizers and persuade them of your value as a speaker. Below is a detailed guide on how to craft a compelling initial application email using a template.

Email Template Structure

Subject Line: Speaker Proposal - [Conference Name] - [Your Topic]
Craft a clear and direct subject line that immediately informs the recipient of the purpose of your email.

Salutation: Dear [Organization/Contact Name],
Personalize the greeting by using the name of the contact or organization wherever possible.

Introduction:
I'm pleased to submit my speaker proposal for the upcoming [Conference Name] scheduled for [dates]. As a [your expertise] specialist, I aim to bring [specific value proposition] to your event.
Introduce yourself and state the purpose of your email

succinctly, emphasizing your area of expertise and the unique value you bring.

Presentation Details:

- **Topic:** [Title]
- **Format:** [Keynote/Workshop/Breakout]
- **Duration:** [Time]
- **Target Audience:** [Specific group]
  Detail the specifics of your presentation, including the format, duration, and the target audience to help the organizers understand how your message fits into their program.

Attachments and Supporting Materials:

- **Professional Headshot:** Enclosed to enhance promotional materials
- **Speaker Bio:** Three versions attached for marketing flexibility
- **Topic Description:** Summary of presentation message and value
- **Learning Objectives:** Compilation of audiences' ket takeaways
- **Video Samples:** Clips to demonstrate style and engagement
- **Client Testimonials:** Feedback highlighting previous successes
- **Engagement Strategies:** Outline participative elements

List all the materials you are attaching to the email. Be clear about what each file contains and how it supports your application.

Personal Connection/Relevance: [Insert a brief statement on how your presentation aligns with the event's theme or organizational goals, or mention any prior connection with the event or the organizers.] Make a personal connection to the event or organization, showing that you have done your homework and are genuinely interested in contributing to their goals.

Closing: I am excited about the opportunity to contribute to [specific aspect of the event or organizational mission] and look forward to potentially enriching your event with meaningful insights and expert knowledge.
Express your enthusiasm about the event and reiterate how you can contribute positively to its success.

Sign-Off: Best regards,
[Your Name]
[Professional Credentials]
[Contact Information]
Close your email formally with all necessary contact information to make it easy for the organizer to reach out to you.

Key Tips

- **Be Concise**: While it's important to include all relevant details, keep your email concise.
- **Customize**: Avoid using a generic template without modifications.
- **Follow-Up**: Consider following up your email with a polite inquiry if you haven't received a response within a reasonable timeframe (about 14 days).

By following this template and guidelines, you can create an effective and professional initial application email that will increase your chances of being selected as a speaker.

2. Online Application Form for Speaking Engagements

The online application form for speakers is streamlined for submission for both event organizers and potential speakers. Here is what you can expect to see on the application form. It's best to have the answers to all of these prompts in another document so you can easily copy and paste the answers into the online form:

SPEAKER APPLICATION FORM

Personal Information
- Full Name: [Text Field]
- Professional Title: [Text Field]
- Company/Organization: [Text Field]
- Email Address: [Email Field]
- Phone Number: [Text Field]
- Professional Website: [URL Field]

Social Media Profiles
- LinkedIn Profile: [URL Field]
- X Handle: [Text Field] (Optional)
- Professional Facebook Page: [URL Field] (Optional)

SPEAKER APPLICATION FORM Cont'd

Speaking Information

- Primary Topic Area: [Dropdown Menu or Text Field]
- Specific Talk Title: [Text Field]
- Target Audience Description: [Text Area]
- Format Preference: [Dropdown Menu - Options: Keynote, Workshop, Both]
- Duration Options: [Dropdown Menu - Example: 30 min, 60 min, 90 min]

SPEAKER APPLICATION FORM Cont'd

Previous Speaking Experience

- Most Recent Event: [Text Field]
- Audience Size: [Number Field]
- Topic Presented: [Text Field]
- Reference Contact: [Text Field - Name and Email]

Additional Information
(Checkboxes to select all that apply)
- ☐ Keynotes
- ☐ Breakouts
- ☐ Panels
- ☐ Interviews
- ☐ Virtuals
- ☐ Emcee

Technical Requirements

- [Text Area - For speakers to list any specific audio/visual needs or other setup requirements]

3. Follow-Up Email Template for Speaker Application

Effective follow-up is crucial in maintaining communication and showing your continued interest in a speaking opportunity. Here's a simple, professional template you can use to follow up on your speaker application for a conference or event.

Email Template Structure

Subject Line: Follow-Up on [Conference Name] Speaker Application – [Your Name]

Email Body:

Dear [Organizer's Name or General Salutation if name is not known],

I hope this message finds you well. I am writing to follow up on my application for a speaking slot at [Conference Name], which I submitted on [Submission Date]. I want to ensure that you have received all the necessary materials and to check on the status of the application process.

Current Status of Application: [Submitted/Pending review]
Materials Provided:

- Professional Bio
- Headshot

- Topic Description
- Video Samples of Past Speaking Engagements
- Client Testimonials

Additional Items Available Upon Request:

- Full Presentation Slides
- Extended & Unedited Video Footage
- Detailed Audience Engagement Plan

I am very enthusiastic about the opportunity to participate in [Conference Name] and am confident that my presentation on [Your Topic] would add significant value to your program.

Please let me know if there is any further information I can provide to assist in your decision-making process. I am looking forward to the possibility of contributing to your event as your speaker, and engaging with your audience.

Thank you very much for considering my application. I hope to hear from you soon.

Best regards,

[Your Full Name]
[Your Professional Title]
[Your Contact Information]
[Your LinkedIn Profile or Professional Website URL]

Tips for Crafting an Effective Follow-Up Email

1. **Be Concise and Clear**: Keep your follow-up email brief. Clearly state the purpose of your email at the beginning to remind the recipient of your previous interaction.
2. **Personalize Your Email**: Whenever possible, address the recipient by first name (name of preference). Personal touches can make your email stand out in a crowded inbox.
3. **Reiterate Your Interest**: Clearly express your enthusiasm for the opportunity. Highlight how your participation could benefit the event, reinforcing the value you bring.
4. **Offer Additional Materials**: Mention any additional materials you can provide to support your application. This shows your preparedness and commitment to the speaking opportunity.
5. **Be Polite and Professional**: Always maintain a polite and professional tone throughout the email. Thank the organizer for considering your application and express your eagerness to receive a response.

By using this follow-up template, you can enhance your communication with event organizers and increase your chances of being selected as a speaker, all while demonstrating professionalism and genuine interest in the opportunity.

Practical Exercises for Enhancing Professional Speaking Applications

These exercises are designed to help professional speakers enhance their application processes, ensuring they present themselves as polished and prepared for any speaking opportunity.

Exercise 1: Application Materials Audit

Objective: Ensure that all application materials are updated, professional, and tailored to showcase your best qualities and relevance to your speaking topics.

Checklist:

1. **Professional Headshot Quality:**
    - Ensure the photo is highest resolution acceptable.
    - Confirm that the attire and backdrop are professional and neutral.
    - Check that the headshot is recent (within the last two years).
2. **Video Presentation Variety:**
    - Assess the diversity of speaking environments shown (conferences, workshops, etc.).
    - Ensure clear audio and video quality.

        - Include clips demonstrating audience engagement and your dynamic speaking style.
3. **Bio Versions Completion:**
        - Have a short (30 words), medium (90 words), and long (150 words) version ready.
        - Ensure each version accurately reflects your current expertise and achievements.
        - Tailor bios to target different audience levels and types.
4. **Topic Description Clarity:**
        - Confirm that your topic descriptions are concise, clear, and compelling.
        - Check for jargon that might be unclear to non-experts.
        - Ensure descriptions reflect how your topic solves specific problems or adds value.
5. **Testimonial Relevance:**
        - Review testimonials to ensure they are relevant to your current speaking topics.
        - Check that they come from credible and respected sources within the industry.
        - Update testimonials to include recent feedback.

Exercise 2: Application Tracking System

Objective: Develop a system to efficiently track and manage your applications, follow-ups, and interactions with event organizers.

System Components:

1. **Application Status Monitoring**:
    - Use a spreadsheet or CRM to track the status of each application (submitted, under review, accepted, rejected).
2. **Follow-Up Schedule Management**:
    - Establish a timeline for follow-ups after you submit your application.
    - Set reminders for sending follow-up communications and checking for responses.
3. **Contact Information Database**:
    - Maintain a database of contact details for event organizers, including names, roles, emails, and phone numbers.
4. **Response Documentation**:
    - Document responses from organizers, including any feedback or requests for additional information.
5. **Opportunity Pipeline**:
    - Track potential future opportunities, including details about upcoming events and application deadlines.

Exercise 3: Communication Template Development

Objective: Create ready-to-use templates for various stages of the application process to streamline communication and maintain professionalism.

Templates:

1. **Initial Applications**:
    - Draft a template covering basic application submissions, including introductions, your value proposition, and attached materials.
2. **Follow-Up Messages**:
    - Develop a follow-up template that politely inquires about the status of your application, reiterates your interest, and offers additional information.
3. **Status Inquiries**:
    - Create a template for more detailed status checks, suitable for use if initial follow-ups receive no response.
4. **Thank You Notes**:
    - Prepare a template for thanking organizers post-event or post-communication, which helps in maintaining good relationships.
5. **Networking Connections**:
    - Develop a networking email template for reaching out to new contacts,

introducing yourself, and proposing potential collaboration or interaction.

Key Takeaways and Action Items

- Regularly audit and update your application materials to ensure they remain relevant and impactful.
- Implement a tracking system to keep your application process organized and timely.
- Use communication templates to maintain consistency and professionalism in all interactions.
- Schedule regular periods to update your materials, review your system efficiency, and refine your communication strategies.

By undertaking these exercises, you'll enhance your ability to manage applications and communicate effectively, demonstrating your professionalism and increasing your chances of being booked for speaking engagements.

Chapter 6: Working with Event Planners

Building strong relationships with event planners is pivotal for a speaking career. They not only provide access to speaking opportunities but also play a crucial role in shaping your reputation within the industry. This chapter delves into understanding event planners, effectively communicating with them, and nurturing long-lasting partnerships.

Understanding Event Planners

Event planners orchestrate the logistical and content-related elements of events, aiming to create memorable and impactful experiences for attendees. Understanding their needs and challenges is the first step toward forming productive relationships.

The Event Planner's Perspective

1. **High-Stakes Environment**: Event planners operate under the pressure of ensuring the event's success, which hinges on the quality and reliability of speakers.
2. **Expectations for Speakers**:
   - **Content Resonance**: Deliver presentations that engage and add value to the audience.
   - **Professionalism**: Exhibit professionalism in all interactions and presentations.
   - **Punctuality**: Meet all deadlines and show up on time for presentations.
   - **Event Contribution**: Enhance the event's reputation through expert delivery and audience interaction.
   - **Measurable Outcomes**: Provide value that can be measured in audience satisfaction and feedback.

Event Planner Priorities - Note the following priorities of event planners:

1. **Risk Reduction**:
   - **Proven Speakers**: Preference for speakers with a track record of success to reduce the risk of poor performance.
   - **Clear Communication**: Value straightforward and timely

communication to avoid misunderstandings and last-minute issues.
    - **Professional Materials**: Need for high-quality promotional materials to facilitate easy marketing and program development.
2. **Value Delivery**:
    - **Content Relevance**: Ensure content is tailored to the audience's interests and the event's theme.
    - **Engagement and Satisfaction**: Seek speakers who can captivate the audience and maintain high engagement levels.
    - **Positive Evaluations**: Aim for speakers whose sessions lead to positive attendee feedback, enhancing the event's success and future attendance.
3. **Process Efficiency**:
    - **Responsiveness**: Appreciate quick and clear responses.
    - **Organized Materials**: Prefer speakers who provide all necessary materials in an organized manner, reducing the need for follow-ups.
    - **Simplified Logistics**: Favor speakers who require minimal special arrangements, making logistical planning more straightforward.

Communicating with Event Planners

Effective communication with event planners can set the foundation for a successful event and potential future opportunities. Here are some key strategies:

1. **Initial Contact**: Be concise yet thorough in your initial query or proposal. Clearly state your expertise, proposed topic, and how it aligns with their event.
2. **During Event Planning**: Maintain open lines of communication. Regularly update planners on your preparation progress and any changes.
3. **Post-Event**: Send a thank-you note expressing your appreciation for the opportunity. Request feedback on your performance and any areas for improvement.

Building Lasting Relationships with Event Planners

1. **Follow-Up**: Regularly check in with event planners you've worked with, sharing updates on your latest topics or speaking engagements that might interest them.
2. **Professional Growth**: Let them know about your new qualifications, awards, or significant projects that could enhance your desirability as a speaker.
3. **Mutual Support**: Offer to assist in promoting the event through your networks or provide

content (like articles or blog posts) that can help boost the event's visibility.
4. **Referrals**: Recommend other reliable speakers or vendors when appropriate, which can be invaluable to event planners and help solidify your relationship.

By understanding and aligning with the needs of event planners, speakers can become indispensable partners in the event planning process, leading to more speaking opportunities and a stronger professional network.

Building the Relationship with Event Planners

Creating a strong and lasting relationship with event planners is crucial for any speaker aiming to enhance their visibility and engagement in the industry. This section offers a detailed approach to developing and maintaining these relationships effectively.

First Impressions

Initial Contact:

- **Professional Correspondence**: Always use a professional tone and format when communicating. Ensure your emails are free

from errors and reflect a respectful and business-like manner.
- **Complete Information Provision**: Provide all the necessary information about your speaking topics, expertise, and experience right from the start. This shows your preparedness and respect for their time.
- **Prompt and Thorough Responses**: Respond quickly to inquiries and requests. This not only shows your professionalism but also your enthusiasm and eagerness to participate.
- **Attention to Their Specific Needs**: Tailor your communication to address the specific themes and goals of their event. Highlight how your presentation can solve problems or enhance the value of their event.

Material Preparation:

- **Organized and Well-Presented**: Submit materials that are not only complete but also organized in a way that makes it easy for planners to review and use.
- **Follows Requested Formats**: Adhere to any specific formatting or submission guidelines provided. This reduces their workload and increases your chances of being selected.
- **Meets or Exceeds Requirements**: Always aim to go beyond the minimum requirements. Providing extra materials like additional case

studies, references, or media clips can make a significant difference.
- **Makes Their Job Easier**: Think about what you can provide that simplifies the event planner's responsibilities, such as ready-to-publish promotional content or pre-prepared social media posts.

Relationship Development

Understanding Their Needs:

- **Ask Clarifying Questions**: Ensure you fully understand their expectations and the scope of the event by asking questions that clarify any ambiguous points.
- **Focus on Their Priorities**: Align your presentation and materials with what is most important to the event's success.
- **Offer Tailored Solutions**: Customize your talk to meet the specific challenges or themes of the event.
- **Demonstrate Flexibility**: Show your willingness to adapt to changes and accommodate last-minute requests if possible.

Managing Expectations:

- **Set Clear Parameters**: Be upfront about what you can deliver to avoid any misunderstandings.

- **Honor Commitments**: Once you have agreed to certain deliverables and timelines, make sure to meet them without fail.
- **Provide Realistic Timelines**: Be honest about how much time you need to prepare and deliver your materials and presentation.
- **Communicate Limitations Professionally**: If certain requests are outside your scope of ability or expertise, communicate this professionally and offer alternative solutions.

By adhering to these guidelines, speakers can cultivate strong, effective relationships with event planners, making them preferred candidates for future opportunities and strong advocates within the industry. These relationships not only help secure more speaking engagements but also foster a network of professionals who might recommend you to others in the field.

Sample Follow-Up Communication with Event Planners

After initial contact, it's essential to maintain communication momentum with event planners. Here's a sample of how you might follow up, 5 calendar days after most recent communication, if you haven't received a response to your initial inquiry or submission.

Subject: Follow-Up: Speaking Opportunity at Leadership Conference 2025

Email Body:

Dear [Perferred name of event planner],

I hope this message finds you well. What is the status of the decision regarding my speaking application for the event [name of event], on [date] in [city]? I know event planners can get busy. My inquiry is to make sure you have all the information you need.

Please let me know what time frame I should expect to hear back from you

Thank you,

[Your Name]
[Professional credentials]
[Contact information]

Tips for Effective Follow-Up Communication

1. **Be Patient but Persistent**: Allow sufficient time between responses to avoid appearing pushy, but also be persistent enough to keep your proposal in consideration.

2. **Be Concise and Focused**: Reiterate your interest and the fit of your presentation for the conference, but keep your message concise.
3. **Add Value**: Each communication should add value or clarify your previous submissions. Consider including new information that might strengthen your application, such as recent speaking engagements or updated materials.
4. **Offer Flexibility**: Show your willingness to adapt to the planner's schedule and needs by offering flexible options for further discussion or providing a self-scheduling link.
5. **Use a Professional Tone**: Maintain a polite and professional tone throughout your communication exchanges to reinforce your professionalism.

By following these practices, you'll enhance your chances of securing speaking opportunities and build strong, productive relationships with event planners.

Communication Template: Confirming Event Specifications with Organizers

When preparing for a speaking engagement, it's essential to communicate your technical and logistical needs to event organizers clearly and effectively. Here's a refined template you can use to ensure that your requirements are well understood and everything is set for a smooth presentation.

Subject Line: Confirmation of Technical and Room Setup Requirements for March 15 Keynote

Email Body:

Dear Jordan,

I hope this message finds you well. As we are nearing the date for the Leadership Conference, I would like to confirm the technical specifications and room setup for my session to ensure everything runs seamlessly on the day.

Presentation Details:

- **Title:** *"Lead Out Loud: Authentic Leadership in Challenging Times"*
- **Date and Time:** March 15, 2025, from 9:00 AM to 10:00 AM
- **Location:** Grand Ballroom

Technical Requirements:

- **Audio:** Wireless lavalier microphone is preferred. I will bring a backup lapel microphone to accommodate any unforeseen issues.
- **Visuals:** A projection system with an HDMI connection is required for the presentation.

- **Sound**: Ability to play audio from a laptop is necessary, as the presentation includes video clips.
- **Control**: I will use my own remote slide advancer and would appreciate a small table near the podium to place materials.

Room Setup Preferences:

- **Visibility**: A confidence monitor on the stage would be greatly beneficial.
- **Layout**: Please arrange the room to allow for easy movement into the audience, fostering interactive engagement.
- **Amenities**: Availability of water on the podium or a nearby table would be appreciated.

Additional Preparations:

- **Equipment Check**: I plan to arrive approximately 90 minutes prior to my session to set up and conduct a thorough tech check.
- **Backup Plans**: My presentation is prepared in 16:9 format with all media tested. Backup slides are available in multiple formats on a USB drive, ensuring smooth delivery even without internet access.

Please review these details and let me know if there are any issues or further requirements needed from my side. I am willing to adjust as needed to fit the technical capabilities and setup of the venue.

Thank you once again for this opportunity. I am looking forward to delivering a valuable and memorable experience for all attendees. I will touch base one week before the event for final confirmations, but feel free to reach out at any time if there are any immediate questions or concerns.

Warm regards,

[Your Name]
[Your Contact Information]
[Day-of-Event Phone Number]

Key Points in Communication

- **Clarity and Detail**: Clearly list each technical and logistical requirement to avoid any unwelcome surprises.
- **Flexibility**: Express willingness to adapt to the venue's capabilities, which helps in maintaining a good relationship with the event organizers.
- **Proactivity**: Confirming details well in advance demonstrates professionalism and helps ensure that the event runs smoothly.
- **Follow-Up**: Planning a final confirmation close to the event date keeps the communication line open and reassures both you and the organizer that everything is on track.

This approach not only facilitates technical and logistical preparations but also reinforces your professionalism and commitment to delivering a high-quality presentation.

Post-Event Follow-Up Email Template

Effective post-event communication is crucial for maintaining relationships with event organizers and setting the stage for future opportunities. This email should be sent no later than 48 hours after your presentation. Here's an enhanced version of a post-event follow-up email that you can use after your speaking engagements.

Subject Line: Heartfelt Thanks and Follow-Up from [Your Presentation Title] at the Leadership Conference

Email Body:

Dear Jordan,

I hope this message finds you well. I wanted to extend my heartfelt thanks for the opportunity to be a part of the Leadership Conference yesterday as your speaker. Engaging with such a proactive and insightful audience was truly an honor, and I am grateful for the professional environment your team created.

Resource Sharing:

- **Leadership Assessment Tool & Guide**: As mentioned during my session, these tools are designed to help attendees implement the strategies discussed. Please find them attached for distribution.
- **Presentation Slides**: For those who requested a copy of the slides, they can be accessed through this secure link: [Insert Secure Link].
- **Custom Article for Newsletter**: Reflecting on the engaging Q&A, I have compiled an article that delves deeper into the key topics we discussed. It's ready for inclusion in your upcoming newsletter, accessible here: [Insert Link].

Event Experience: The organization of the conference was impeccable, and the engagement from the attendees was a testament to the quality of your events. The technical setup was flawlessly executed, which facilitated a highly interactive session. Please convey my appreciation to everyone involved.

Ongoing Support: Should there be any further questions or discussions prompted by my session, I am at your full disposal to provide additional insights or information.

Feedback Request: Gathering insights from attendee evaluations is vital for my continuous improvement.

When convenient, I would greatly appreciate any feedback on my session. This invaluable information will guide enhancements to my future presentations.

Future Collaboration: Thank you once again for a memorable experience. I am eager to explore further opportunities to contribute to your organization's objectives, be it future conferences or other formats needing a speaker.

Please do not hesitate to reach out if there's any additional way I can support your team or participate in upcoming projects.

Warm regards,

[Your Name]
[Your Professional Credentials]
[Your Contact Information]
[Your LinkedIn Profile or Professional Website URL]

Tips for Maximizing Post-Event Email Impact

1. **Personalize Your Message**: Tailor your email to reflect specific experiences at the event. Mentioning details shows your genuine engagement and appreciation.
2. **Provide Value**: Attach useful resources or additional content that benefit the event

attendees. This reinforces your commitment to providing ongoing value beyond your session.
3. **Seek Feedback**: Explicitly asking for feedback demonstrates your dedication to professional growth and shows that you value the organizer's opinion.
4. **Open Doors for Future Opportunities**: Expressing your willingness to collaborate further encourages the organizer to consider you for future events and can lead to more speaking opportunities.

By following these guidelines, you can effectively communicate your appreciation, reinforce your professional relationships, and set the stage for future engagements.

Relationship Maintenance Email Template

Keeping in touch with event planners and industry contacts, 90 days after your presentation, through thoughtful communication can strengthen your professional relationships and keep you top-of-mind for future opportunities. Here's an enhanced template for an email that nurtures these connections by sharing relevant insights and extending a personal touch.

In my previous book "Lead Out Loud. Keys to Unlock Your Professional Excellence", I introduced the 4 communication LEAD™ styles: Laid back, Energetic, Analytical, and Direct. Here are 4 different email templates depending on the event planner's communication style:

Laid Back

Hello Larry, I hope the (something specific from the last correspondence) is going well! This email is to see if there are any questions you might have thought of since my submission proposal (insert time frame). I want to keep my calendar clear for you. How soon should I expect to hear from you?

Energetic

Hello Elizabeth!! How are things going in your wonderful city of (City)? Just realized that (Time Frame) has gone by, and I have not heard back from you. My apologies for any delay. I am excited about the continuation of our discussion to be your speaker. Great news! [The Date of Their Event] is still available on my calendar. I can hold it for you until GIVE A DATE. What time frame should I expect to hear back from you about confirmation?

Analytical

Hello Alex. Regarding the proposal I submitted to be your speaker for:

- EVENT
- DATE
- TIME
- LOCATION
- TOPIC

Within what time frame should I anticipate hearing back from you? Also, will the correspondence be by email, phone, or text? Thank you. If you want to have additional correspondence before making your decision, please contact me at: PHONE, EMAIL, or SCHEDULING LINK.

Direct

Hello Dawn. How soon are you making your speaker selection for the EVENT on DATE, IN LOCATION?

Tips for Crafting Effective Relationship Maintenance Communication

1. **Be Relevant**: Share content or insights that are directly relevant to the recipient's work or recent discussions. This shows that you are attentive and value the relationship beyond just professional opportunities.
2. **Be Personal**: Whenever possible, add a personal touch by recalling specific details about your

interactions or by mentioning upcoming opportunities to provide value.
3. **Be Supportive**: Offer resources or information that can help them in their role. This positions you as a valuable and supportive contact.
4. **Be Engaging**: Invite further communication to discuss shared interests or potential collaborations. This can reinforce your relationship and open doors to new opportunities.

By utilizing these strategies, you can maintain and enhance your professional relationships effectively, ensuring a network that's engaged and mutually beneficial

Managing Speaker Applications and Responses

Effectively managing responses from event planners and maintaining a detailed database of interactions can significantly enhance a speaker's ability to secure future engagements and build lasting professional relationships. Here's a guide to handling various types of responses and managing your contacts effectively.

Response Handling

Types of Responses:

1. **Automated Confirmations**: These are standard acknowledgments that your application has been received. While generic, they confirm that your speaking proposal is in the review process.
2. **Selection Notifications**: Notifications that you have been chosen to speak. These require prompt and professional follow-up to confirm details and begin event preparation.
3. **Follow-up Correspondence**: Requests for additional information or clarification. Responding quickly and thoroughly demonstrates professionalism.
4. **Rejection Notices**: Informing you that you have not been selected. Handle these gracefully and seek feedback if appropriate.

Response Strategies:

- **Positive Acceptance**: Confirm your participation enthusiastically, and clarify any immediate next steps, such as signing contracts or providing additional materials.
- **Professional Follow-through**: For all types of positive follow-ups, ensure you meet all requested requirements on time and maintain open lines of communication.

- **Graceful Rejection Handling**: Thank the organizers for the opportunity to apply, express your hope to be considered for future events, and inquire about ways to improve your proposals for future opportunities.
- **Relationship Maintenance**: Regardless of the outcome, aim to maintain communication with the organizers. Sending periodic updates about your work or insights relevant to their industry can keep you on their radar for future opportunities.

Database Management

Contact Information:

- Maintain up-to-date contact details for event planners and organizers, including names, titles, phone numbers, and email addresses.

Detailed Planner Records:

- Keep records of each planner's preferences and past communications. Note any personal details they share (e.g., interests, birthday) which can be used to personalize future communications.

Organization Information:

- Document details about the organization, such as size, industry focus, and previous events, to tailor your proposals and communications effectively.

Event Histories:

- Track your history of applications with each organization, including which topics were submitted, the response received, and any feedback provided.

Relationship Notes:

- Keep notes on any personal connections or conversations that can inform how you communicate with them in the future.

Follow-up Systems

Scheduled Check-ins:

- Establish a routine for reaching out to key contacts, whether semi-annually or after major industry events, to keep your name fresh and demonstrate continued interest in collaboration.

Value-added Communication:

- Share articles, studies, or other content that is relevant to their business or past events. This shows you understand their needs and are proactive about providing value.

Personalized Outreach:

- Tailor your communication based on the relationship history and any personal interests of the contact to strengthen the connection.

Long-term Relationship Building:

- View each interaction as a step in a long-term relationship. Even if a particular application does not result in a speaking engagement, maintaining a positive relationship can lead to future opportunities.

By strategically managing your applications and responses and maintaining a detailed database, you can increase your chances of being selected for speaking opportunities and also build a network of professional contacts that can advocate for you throughout your career.

Delivering Value Beyond Speaking

As a professional speaker, providing value beyond the actual speaking engagement can significantly enhance your reputation and open doors to new opportunities. Here are ways you can add value before, during, and after an event.

Pre-Event Support

Marketing Assistance:

- **Promotional Materials**: Provide high-quality photos, videos, and descriptive content about your presentation that can be used in marketing materials.
- **Social Media Support**: Engage with the event's social media channels by sharing and promoting the event, and encourage your followers to attend.
- **Pre-Event Promotion**: Participate in interviews, webinars, or live Q&A sessions to build excitement and attendance for the event.
- **Testimonials and Endorsements**: Offer testimonials from past events to boost credibility and trust among potential attendees.

Content Customization:

- **Audience Research Collaboration**: Work with the event planners to understand the audience demographics and their needs to tailor your content effectively.
- **Material Adaptation**: Customize your presentations to address the specific issues and challenges relevant to the audience.

- **Targeted Examples and Applications**: Use case studies or examples that resonate specifically with the event's demographic.
- **Specialized Handouts or Resources**: Provide handouts, digital resources, or tools that attendees can use to implement what they learn.

Post-Event Excellence

Follow-Up Process:

- **Thank You Communications**: Send personalized thank-you notes to the event organizers and key participants.
- **Feedback Collection**: Request feedback on your session to gauge its impact and look for areas to improve.
- **Resource Provision**: Offer additional resources post-event to help attendees implement key takeaways.
- **Continued Availability**: Let participants know how they can keep in touch, whether for questions, further learning, or professional services.

Evaluation Enhancement:

- **Encouraging Positive Feedback**: Motivate satisfied attendees to leave positive feedback on social media or event feedback forms.
- **Addressing Concerns Professionally**: Respond constructively to any negative feedback and offer to address unresolved issues.
- **Implementing Improvements**: Use feedback to refine and improve your future presentations.
- **Documenting Successes**: Maintain a portfolio of success stories and positive outcomes from your talks to use in marketing and promotion.

Referral Facilitation:

- **Making Connection Introductions**: Help connect attendees or organizers with other professionals in your network, adding value to their professional lives.
- **Providing Testimonials**: Offer to provide testimonials for the event or for key staff members, which they can use for their marketing efforts.
- **Recommending for Other Events**: If you know of other events where the organizers or participants could be a good fit, make recommendations.
- **Expanding Their Professional Network**: Introduce them to others in your network to help expand their reach and opportunities.

By focusing on delivering value beyond just the presentation itself, you build stronger relationships with event organizers and attendees, establish your reputation as a thoughtful and effective speaker, and increase your chances of being invited back or recommended for other speaking opportunities. This comprehensive approach ensures that your professional impact extends far beyond the stage.

Case Studies

Case Study 1: The Reliable Professional

Margaret's approach to her speaking engagement at the National Coalition for Family Safety's annual conference exemplifies several best practices for speakers aiming to build lasting relationships with event planners and broaden their professional opportunities. Here's an analysis of what Margaret did right and why her strategies were so effective:

Pre-Event Excellence

1. **Early Material Submission**:
    - **Impact**: By submitting her materials well ahead of the deadline, Margaret

ensured that the event team had ample time to review and utilize her resources effectively.
    - **Lesson**: Proactivity can set you apart from other speakers. It shows that you respect the planner's time and are committed to contributing to the event's success.
2. **Providing Promotional Materials**:
    - **Impact**: The promotional video and complete package enabled the event team to feature Margaret prominently in their marketing, increasing attendance at her session.
    - **Lesson**: Going beyond the minimum requirements can significantly enhance your visibility and the event's marketing efforts.

During the Event

1. **Early Arrival and Venue Familiarization**:
    - **Impact**: Arriving early allowed Margaret to adjust her session to fit the venue's unique layout, ensuring that her presentation was delivered effectively.
    - **Lesson**: Familiarizing yourself with the event space can prevent unforeseen

challenges and show your dedication to a seamless presentation.
2. **Networking with Key Individuals**:
   - **Impact**: By introducing herself to the technical staff and board members, Margaret expanded her network within the organization, which is crucial for future opportunities.
   - **Lesson**: Effective networking at events can lead to additional bookings and deeper professional relationships.

Post-Event Follow-Up

1. **Prompt Delivery of Promised Materials and Feedback**:
   - **Impact**: Margaret's quick follow-up with additional resources and a comprehensive report on audience engagement demonstrated her commitment to providing value beyond her talk.
   - **Lesson**: Timely and thorough follow-ups show that you care about the lasting impact of your presentation and support the event's goals.
2. **Personalized Thank You Notes**:
   - **Impact**: Sending personalized notes to each planning team member

personalized her interactions, making her memorable and appreciated.
- **Lesson**: A small gesture of gratitude can solidify a positive impression and encourage planners to consider you for future events.

Long-Term Results

Margaret's strategic approach ensured her immediate success at the conference and also paved the way for future engagements through recommendations and repeat bookings. Her story illustrates the profound impact that thorough preparation, proactive communication, and thoughtful follow-up can have on a speaker's career.

Key Takeaways

- **Professionalism at Every Step**: Event planners value speakers who are easy to work with and who consistently deliver high-quality interactions.
- **Build Trust Through Reliability**: Demonstrating reliability in every aspect of the event process makes you a preferred choice for future speaking opportunities.
- **Maximize Every Interaction**: From technical preparations to networking, every interaction at an event can contribute to your success and

should be approached with intention and professionalism.

By adopting Margaret's meticulous and considerate approach, speakers can significantly enhance their professional reputation and develop beneficial relationships with event planners, leading to more speaking opportunities and career growth.

Case Study 2: The Problem Solver - Turning Crisis into Opportunity

Rebecca's swift and effective response to an urgent request for a substitute speaker at the Healthcare Management Summit exemplifies how adaptability and professionalism can turn a potential crisis into a significant career opportunity. Here's an analysis of her approach and the factors contributing to her success.

Swift and Strategic Response

1. **Immediate Availability**: Rebecca's quick reply to the urgent request demonstrated her readiness and eagerness to step in, setting a positive tone from the start.
    - **Lesson**: Responsiveness to opportunities, especially time-sensitive

ones, can set you apart in a competitive field.
2. **Solution-Oriented Communication**: Her email was a statement of availability; it was a comprehensive package that reassured the event organizer of her capability to handle the situation.
   - **Lesson**: Providing a clear, concise plan with relevant materials (like past talk videos and testimonials) can greatly increase the event planner's confidence in your abilities.

Customized and Informed Preparation

1. **Content Adaptation**: Rebecca spent the night customizing her presentation to fit the specific audience of healthcare executives, demonstrating her commitment to delivering value.
   - **Lesson**: Tailoring content to meet the specific needs of the audience enhances engagement and also cements your reputation as a thoughtful and adaptable speaker.
2. **Pre-Event Collaboration**: Her proactive approach to collaborating with the conference director and planning team helped integrate her session seamlessly into the event's agenda.
   - **Lesson**: Collaborating closely with event organizers ensures that your

presentation aligns well with the overall event and enhances the experience for attendees.

Exceeding Expectations

1. **Early Arrival and Technical Preparation**: By arriving early and handling all technical preparations meticulously, Rebecca ensured a professional presentation delivery.
    - **Lesson**: Taking charge of logistical details can alleviate stress for event organizers and contribute to a smoother execution of your session.
2. **Supplemental Materials**: Providing additional handouts and offering a follow-up survey for attendees went beyond the expected, adding significant value to her contribution.
    - **Lesson**: Offering more than what's expected can leave a lasting impression on both the audience and the event organizers.

Effective Follow-Up

1. **Post-Event Communication**: Rebecca's thoughtful follow-up with the conference director included additional resources and an offer to address any further questions from attendees.

- **Lesson**: Effective follow-up communication reinforces your professional image and shows your dedication to the event's long-term success.
2. **Building on the Experience**: Her readiness to assist and the quality of her delivery solved an immediate problem and also opened doors for future engagements through recommendations.
    - **Lesson**: Delivering excellent content under pressure can lead to more opportunities and serve as a powerful testimonial to your capabilities.

Outcome

Rebecca's proactive and exemplary handling of the situation salvaged the conference session and also significantly expanded her professional network and led to subsequent speaking opportunities. This case study highlights the importance of readiness, adaptability, and thorough professionalism in capitalizing on unexpected opportunities in the speaking industry.

By adopting Rebecca's strategies, speakers can enhance their ability to manage crises, exceed client expectations, and build rewarding professional relationships that extend well beyond a single event.

Case Study 3: The Relationship Builder - From One-Time Speaker to Trusted Advisor

Camille's approach to her speaking engagement exemplifies how a speaker can transcend the role of a presenter to become a trusted advisor and a valuable partner. Here's a breakdown of her strategic actions and their implications for building enduring professional relationships.

Pre-Event Engagement

1. **Personalized Video Message**:
    - **Impact**: This introduction personalized her communication and also demonstrated genuine interest in the event's success beyond her session.
    - **Lesson**: Personal touches can differentiate you from other speakers and initiate a rapport that goes beyond standard professional boundaries.
2. **Understanding Organizer Needs**:
    - **Impact**: Asking about the event planner's goals and challenges showed that Camille was committed to contributing positively to the event as a whole.
    - **Lesson**: Understanding and aligning with the event planner's objectives can

make you a more effective and appreciated contributor.
3. **Proactive Solutions**:
    - **Impact**: By offering to handle potential logistical issues proactively, Camille alleviated the planner's workload and pre-empted common event-day problems.
    - **Lesson**: Demonstrating initiative and self-sufficiency makes you a less burdensome and a more appealing choice for event planners.

During the Event

1. **Active Conference Participation**:
    - **Impact**: Camille's involvement in the conference beyond her scheduled talk, such as assisting attendees, enriched the event experience for everyone.
    - **Lesson**: Being helpful and engaged throughout the event can increase your visibility and endear you to both attendees and organizers.
2. **Content Integration and Promotion**:
    - **Impact**: By connecting her talk to other aspects of the conference and promoting exhibitors, Camille created added value

for the organizers and other participants.
  - **Lesson**: Showing that you care about the event's overall success, not just your session, can make you a standout speaker.

Post-Event Development

1. **Comprehensive Follow-Up**:
   - **Impact**: Her detailed session report and additional resources helped extend the impact of her presentation and demonstrated her thoroughness and professionalism.
   - **Lesson**: Effective follow-up can solidify your reputation as a detail-oriented and thoughtful professional.
2. **Ongoing Engagement**:
   - **Impact**: Regularly sharing useful content and personal gestures like gifting a book showed that her commitment to the relationship extended beyond the event.
   - **Lesson**: Maintaining contact and continuing to provide value without immediate expectation of return can transform professional relationships into partnerships.

Long-Term Results

1. **Trusted Advisor Role:**
   - **Impact**: Camille's ongoing engagement and consistent delivery of value led to her becoming a trusted advisor, not just a recurring speaker.
   - **Lesson**: Building trust through consistent, high-quality interactions can lead to more significant roles and responsibilities within organizations.
2. **Expanding Professional Opportunities**:
   - **Impact**: This relationship not only secured more speaking engagements but also consulting opportunities and introductions to other event planners.
   - **Lesson**: A strong relationship with one event planner can lead to a network of opportunities, leveraging their trust and endorsement.

Key Takeaways

Camille's case study illustrates that a speaker's role doesn't end when the microphone is turned off. Continuous engagement, providing actionable solutions, and genuine interest in the event's success are pivotal in evolving from a service provider to a valued partner. This approach enhances the speaker's career and contributes to the event's value, creating a win-win scenario.

Practical Exercises for Building Relationships with Event Planners

These exercises are designed to help speakers enhance their relationships with event planners by developing a deeper understanding of their needs and expectations, improving communication strategies, and articulating their value effectively.

Exercise 1: Event Planner Profile

Creating detailed profiles for event planners can help tailor your communication and presentations to better meet their specific needs.

Steps:

1. **Collect Information**: Research the professional background of event planners you're working with or wish to work with. This might include their career path, key successes, and the types of events they typically manage
2. **Understand Preferences**: Note their preferred methods of communication (e.g., email, phone, social media) and response times. Adjust your communication style to suit their preferences.
3. **Identify Priorities**: Learn what is most important to them in their role—perhaps reducing risk, increasing attendee satisfaction,

or ensuring educational content is cutting-edge.
4. **Review Past Events**: Analyze events they have previously managed to understand the scope, style, and outcomes they favor.
5. **Decision-making Factors**: Determine what factors influence their decisions to hire speakers, such as budget constraints, speaker expertise, or audience feedback.

Exercise 2: Communication Audit

Regularly auditing your communication methods can ensure you maintain professionalism and efficiency in your interactions with event planners.

Steps:

1. **Email Professionalism**: Review your email templates and past emails for clarity, tone, and professionalism. Ensure you use a professional signature and clear subject lines.
2. **Response Times**: Evaluate how quickly you respond to correspondence. Setting a standard for timely responses can improve your reliability as a contact.
3. **Follow-up Consistency**: Check how consistently you follow up with contacts. Implement a system to remind you when to send follow-up emails or calls.

4. **Organization Systems**: Assess your current methods for organizing contact information, notes from meetings, and past communications. Consider using a CRM system if not already doing so.
5. **Accessibility**: Make sure you are easily accessible to event planners. This might mean having a clear contact strategy on your website or maintaining active professional social media profiles.

Exercise 3: Value Proposition Development

Crafting specific value propositions for different types of event planners can help articulate how you can uniquely address their needs.

Steps:

1. **Corporate Event Managers**: Focus on how your speaking can enhance corporate goals, such as improving employee morale, leadership skills, or industry knowledge.
2. **Association Conference Planners**: Emphasize your ability to attract attendees by aligning with the association's mission and increasing member engagement.
3. **Educational Institution Coordinators**: Highlight your educational content's relevance and impact on students' or professionals' continuing education.

4. **Non-profit Organization Directors**: Demonstrate understanding of non-profit budgets and how your talks can aid in fundraising efforts or community outreach.

Key Takeaways

- **Understand the Planner**: The more you know about the event planner's preferences and challenges, the better you can serve their needs and become a preferred speaker.
- **Communicate Effectively**: Professionalism in communication reassures event planners of your reliability and suitability for their events.
- **Customized Value**: Directly addressing the specific needs of different types of event planners with tailored value propositions can set you apart from other speakers.

Action Items

- **Implement Profiles**: Start building and maintaining detailed profiles for each event planner with whom you interact.
- **Enhance Communications**: Refine your communication strategies based on your audit findings.
- **Establish Protocols**: Develop and standardize follow-up protocols to ensure consistent and valuable interactions.

- **Use Technology**: Utilize technology like scheduling apps and electronic contracts to keep track of interactions, preferences, and key information about event planners.

By focusing on these areas, speakers can cultivate more meaningful and productive relationships with event planners. This leads to more engagement opportunities and a stronger professional network.

Conclusion:

As professional speakers, we are more than problem speakers; we have to be problem solvers. Our biggest value as speakers is to use storytelling, research, and content to make a positive difference in our audiences. Seed... fruit.. Fertile soil... blossom... be sure to always be prepared to give your audience what they deserve, which is your professional best.

Amplify with Vincent:

www.VincentPhipps.com

Appendix A: Speaker Application Checklist

Introduction: This checklist is designed to help speakers prepare and organize the essential materials needed for speaking opportunities. By having these items ready and up-to-date, speakers can efficiently respond to invitations and application deadlines, presenting themselves as professional and prepared candidates.

Essential Materials Checklist

Professional Identity

- ☐ **Business Name**: Ensure you have a legally established name for professional use.
- ☐ **Professional Email Address**: Use a domain-specific email address that conveys professionalism.
- ☐ **Business Phone Number**: Have a dedicated number for business communication.
- ☐ **Professional Website**: Maintain a current website with relevant content about your speaking engagements.

- ☐ **Social Media Profiles**: Keep active profiles, particularly on professional networks like LinkedIn.
- ☐ **Business Cards**: Design and print up-to-date business cards.
- ☐ **Speaker One-Sheet**: Create a compelling one-sheet document that summarizes your speaking credentials and offerings.

Headshots and Visual Materials

- ☐ **Professional Headshot**: Have a high-resolution headshot in both portrait and landscape orientations.
- ☐ **Alternate Images**: Include other professional images for different contexts.
- ☐ **Action Shots**: Provide photos of you speaking at events.
- ☐ **Logo Files**: Keep various formats of your logo for different uses.
- ☐ **Branded Presentation Template**: Design a template that reflects your brand for consistency.
- ☐ **Stage/Backdrop Requirements**: Document your preferred presentation settings and backdrop requirements.

Bio Versions

- ☐ **Short Bio**: A 30-word bio for quick introductions
- ☐ **Standard Bio**: A 90-word bio for programs and announcements
- ☐ **Full Bio**: A 150-word bio for detailed contexts like websites and press kits
- ☐ **Industry-specific Bio Variations**: Tailor bios to specific industries if applicable
- ☐ **Third-person and First-person Versions**: Prepare bios in both narrative voices for different uses
- ☐ **Audio/Video Introduction Script**: Script your self-introduction for videos or live presentations.

Topic Development

- ☐ **Primary Topic Titles**: Develop 3-5 variations to cater to different audiences or event themes.
- ☐ **Secondary/Alternate Titles**: Have ready alternatives for different contexts.
- ☐ **Content Summaries**: Write summaries (100-200 words) for each topic.
- ☐ **Learning Objectives**: Define clear and measurable learning objectives for each presentation.

- ☐ **Topic Categories/Keywords**: Identify relevant categories and keywords for your topics.
- ☐ **Customization Options**: Document how each topic can be tailored to specific audiences or events.

Video and Audio Materials

- ☐ **Speaker Demo Video**: A professional 3-5 minute compilation of speaking highlights
- ☐ **Full Presentation Recordings**: Keep recordings of full sessions for review or distribution
- ☐ **Testimonial Clips**: Short video clips from clients or audience members
- ☐ **Brief Topic Introduction Videos**: Videos introducing key topics or themes
- ☐ **Audio Samples**: Clips of spoken content, such as podcast interviews or presentations
- ☐ **Podcast Interviews**: Participate in or host podcast sessions relevant to your expertise

Supplementary Materials

- ☐ **Client Testimonials**: Gather and organize written testimonials from clients.
- ☐ **Case Studies**: Develop detailed case studies that showcase your impact.

- ☐ **Published Articles/Books**: Keep a portfolio of your published work.
- ☐ **Media Appearances**: Document any appearances on television, radio, or online media.
- ☐ **Awards and Recognition**: Compile any professional recognitions or awards.
- ☐ **Professional Credentials/Certifications**: Maintain current records of your qualifications and certifications.

By using this checklist, speakers can ensure they have a robust portfolio of materials that showcase their expertise and professionalism and also facilitate quick and effective responses to speaking opportunities. This preparedness enhances a speaker's professionalism and can significantly influence their success in securing speaking engagements.

Application Process Checklist

This checklist provides a structured approach for speakers applying to various events, ensuring they present a polished and professional application that aligns with specific event requirements. Following these steps will help maximize your chances of being selected and maintain a well-organized approach to application management.

Pre-Application Research

- ☐ **Research Organization and Event**: Understand the history, mission, and past events organized by the host.
- ☐ **Review Past Speakers and Topics**: Analyze themes and topics from previous years to tailor your proposal.
- ☐ **Identify Target Audience Demographics**: Adjust your presentation style and content to match audience expectations.
- ☐ **Understand Event Theme and Objectives**: Align your topic to support the overarching goals of the event.
- ☐ **Review Application Requirements Thoroughly**: Ensure understanding of all necessary components for the application.
- ☐ **Note Submission Deadlines**: Document and set reminders for all relevant deadlines.
- ☐ **Identify Decision-Makers**: Know who is responsible for speaker selection to tailor communications.

Application Materials Compilation

- ☐ **Customize Topic Title for Specific Event**: Adjust your topic title to resonate with the event's theme and focus.
- ☐ **Adapt Content Summary for Target Audience**: Rewrite your content summary to address the specific interests and needs of the audience.
- ☐ **Align Learning Objectives with Event Goals**: Ensure your learning objectives support the event's educational aims.
- ☐ **Select Appropriate Bio Version**: Choose the bio length and focus that best suits the event's format.
- ☐ **Choose Relevant Testimonials**: Include testimonials that reflect your suitability and impact for similar events.
- ☐ **Select Appropriate Video Materials**: Provide video clips that showcase your effectiveness as a speaker in contexts similar to the event.
- ☐ **Prepare Additional Requested Materials**: Compile any extra materials such as slides, outlines, or handouts as specified.

Submission Process

- ☐ **Complete All Required Fields**: Fill out every section of the application form without leaving blanks.
- ☐ **Double-check Word Counts/Character Limits**: Ensure all text meets the specified parameters.
- ☐ **Proofread All Materials**: Check for typos, grammatical errors, and clarity in communication.
- ☐ **Verify File Formats and Sizes**: Ensure all attachments meet the technical requirements.
- ☐ **Test All Links and Attachments**: Confirm that all hyperlinks and attached files open correctly.
- ☐ **Save Confirmation/Receipt Information**: Keep a record of submission confirmations or receipts.
- ☐ **Document Submission Date and Method**: Note how and when the application was submitted.
- ☐ **Track Login Credentials**: Store usernames, passwords, and portal URLs securely.
- ☐ **Schedule Follow-Up Date**: Set a reminder to follow up if you haven't heard back by a specific date.

Follow-Up Protocol

- ☐ **Send Confirmation Inquiry**: If no automatic response is received, confirm that your application was submitted successfully.
- ☐ **Schedule Periodic Status Checks**: Regularly inquire about the status of your application, respecting the selection timeline.
- ☐ **Prepare for Interview/Discussion Requests**: Be ready to participate in further discussions or interviews as part of the selection process.
- ☐ **Document All Communication**: Keep records of all interactions with the event organizers.
- ☐ **Save Selection Notification**: Archive any notifications regarding your application status.
- ☐ **Respond to Acceptance or Rejection Professionally**: Reply courteously to all decisions, seeking feedback if rejected.
- ☐ **Update Speaking Calendar**: Adjust your professional calendar based on the outcomes of your applications.

By systematically following this checklist, speakers can ensure a thorough, timely, and organized approach to applying for speaking opportunities. This increases the likelihood of success and establishes professional relationships with event organizers.

Event Preparation Checklist

This comprehensive checklist is designed to ensure all aspects of event participation are covered, from contract agreements to logistical arrangements and promotional efforts. Following this checklist will help speakers prepare effectively for their engagements and ensure a smooth, professional experience for both themselves and the event organizers.

Contract and Terms

1. **Review and Sign Contract**:
    - Thoroughly read and understand the terms before signing to avoid any misunderstandings.
2. **Confirm Date, Time, and Location**:
    - Double-check these fundamental details to ensure accuracy in your planning.
3. **Verify Speaking Fee and Payment Terms**:
    - Ensure clarity on the amount, invoicing process, and payment schedule.
4. **Understand Cancellation Policy**:
    - Know the conditions under which you or the event organizer can cancel, and the penalties or refunds involved.
5. **Clarify Travel and Accommodation Arrangements**:

- Confirm if arrangements are handled by the organizer or if you need to book them yourself, and who covers the costs.
6. **Confirm Recording/Distribution Rights**:
    - Understand what rights the organizer has to record and distribute your presentation and any royalties or restrictions.
7. **Review Any Non-Compete Clauses**:
    - Check for any clauses that restrict your participation in other events or engagements.

Logistical Preparation

1. **Communicate Technical Requirements**:
    - Provide a detailed list of your technical needs to the event organizer well in advance.
2. **Confirm Room Setup Preferences**:
    - Discuss and confirm the layout and setup of the venue to suit your presentation style.
3. **Verify Audiovisual Equipment**:
    - Ensure all necessary AV equipment is available and meets your specifications.
4. **Arrange Travel Logistics**:
    - Plan and book travel itineraries, including flights, accommodations, and local transport.
5. **Schedule Rehearsal/Technical Check Time**:

- Arrange a specific time with the venue to test all equipment and walkthrough your presentation.
6. **Prepare Backup Materials and Equipment**:
    - Bring backups for critical components like slides, batteries, adapters, and cables.
7. **Create Day-of-Event Schedule**:
    - Outline your activities and timings for the event day to stay organized and on time.

Promotional Support

1. **Provide Requested Marketing Materials**:
    - Supply the organizer with high-quality images, bios, and other materials for promotional use.
2. **Share Event on Social Media**:
    - Promote the event through your social media channels to increase attendance and engagement.
3. **Prepare Pre-Event Content**:
    - Develop content such as blog posts, videos, or articles to build interest and momentum before the event.
4. **Arrange Media Interviews If Applicable**:
    - Coordinate with the organizer's PR team to schedule interviews to further promote the event.
5. **Create Event-Specific Handouts**:

- Design handouts that provide added value to your session and leave a lasting impression.
6. **Design Supplementary Resources**:
    - Develop additional resources like worksheets, guides, or follow-up readings that attendees can use after the event.
7. **Schedule Post-Event Follow-Up**:
    - Plan how you will engage with attendees after the event, such as thank you emails, feedback surveys, or offers related to your services.

By systematically addressing each item on this checklist, speakers can ensure they are well-prepared and can focus on delivering a compelling and valuable presentation. This preparation also demonstrates professionalism and dedication to both the event organizers and the audience, enhancing the speaker's reputation and potential for future engagements.

Application Tracking Templates

These templates are designed to help speakers manage and monitor their speaking engagements and application efforts. By using these templates, you can maintain organized records of your applications, track your communication with event organizers, and evaluate the return on investment for your engagements.

1. Comprehensive Opportunity Tracker
This template helps track each opportunity from initial contact to final follow-up:

Event Name	Organization	Contact Person	Event Date	Application Deadline	Date Submitted	Fee Range	Location	Notes
Example Event	ABC Conference	John Doe jdoe@example.com 555-555-5555	10/15/25	8/1/2025	7/25/2025	$2,000-$5,000	City, State	Any other additional info

This tracking template is invaluable for maintaining a structured approach to managing speaking engagements and analyzing their success. They help ensure that all aspects of each opportunity are considered and evaluated, leading to more informed decisions and strategic career management.

Troubleshooting Common Application Challenges

When applying for speaking opportunities, you may encounter various challenges that can hinder your ability to secure engagements. Here are common issues and effective strategies for addressing them to ensure your application process runs smoothly.

Challenge: Missing Application Confirmation

Symptoms:

- No confirmation email after submission
- Uncertainty if the application was received
- No response to initial inquiry

Solutions:

1. **Wait 24-48 Hours:** Some systems send batch confirmations, so it may take time before you receive a response.
2. **Check Spam/Junk Folder:** Important emails can sometimes be filtered out of your main inbox. Regularly check your spam or junk folder.
3. **Send a Professional Follow-Up Email:**
    - **Subject:** Confirming Receipt of Speaking Proposal - [Event Name]
- **Email Body:**

Dear [Name],

I submitted my speaking proposal for [Event Name] on [date], but I have yet to receive confirmation that the proposal was received. With your deadline of [deadline date] approaching, I want to ensure my materials are received properly.

Could you please confirm receipt of my submission for [presentation title]?

Thank you for your assistance.

Best regards,

[Your Name]

4. **Call the Main Office**: If there's no response to your email, consider calling the event organizer's office to confirm receipt.
5. **Check Application Portal**: If the event uses an online application system, log in to check the status of your submission.

Prevention:

- **Take Screenshots**: Capture screenshots of submission confirmations for your records.
- **Note Confirmation Numbers**: Keep a record of any confirmation numbers or transaction IDs.
- **Save Copies of All Submitted Materials**: Have backups of all documents and forms submitted.
- **Use Trackable Email Services**: Consider using email services that confirm when your email has been opened.

Additional Tips for Application Challenges

Technical Issues with Submission Portals:

- **Test the System**: If possible, try submitting a partial application to identify any bugs or issues.
- **Contact Support**: Reach out to technical support for the application system if you encounter persistent issues.

Lost or Misplaced Materials:

- **Regular Updates**: Regularly update and back up your application materials to avoid losses.
- **Cloud Storage**: Use cloud storage solutions to keep an accessible copy of all application documents.

Unclear Application Requirements:

- **Seek Clarifications**: Contact the event organizers directly if the application instructions are unclear.
- **Attend Information Sessions**: If available, attend webinars or Q&A sessions about the application process.

By implementing these strategies, you can navigate common application challenges more effectively and increase your chances of being selected for speaking opportunities. Always maintain a proactive approach and be prepared to adapt as necessary to ensure your applications are received and considered by event organizers.

Challenge: Troubleshooting Technical Issues During Submission

When applying for speaking opportunities, technical glitches can be a significant barrier. Here's how to effectively address and prevent these issues to ensure your application process is not disrupted.

Symptoms of Technical Issues

- **Website Crashes During Submission**: The application portal becomes unresponsive or shuts down.
- **Error Messages When Uploading Materials**: Pop-ups indicate failures during file upload.
- **Form Reset Losing Information**: Data entered in form fields is lost unexpectedly.
- **Files Rejected Due to Size/Format Issues**: Uploads do not complete because files do not meet the specified requirements.

Solutions to Technical Issues

1. **Use Different Browsers**: If one browser fails, try another (e.g., Chrome, Firefox, Safari) to see if the issue persists across platforms.
2. **Clear Browser Cache and Cookies**: Sometimes, clearing your browser's cache and cookies can resolve loading or performance issues.
3. **Reduce File Sizes**:
    - **Compress Images**: Use tools to reduce image resolution to 72 dpi, suitable for web use.
    - **File Compression Tools**: Reduce the size of PDFs or other documents with software designed for compression.
    - **Split Large Files**: If possible, divide larger files into smaller, manageable parts.
    - **Convert Files to Standard Formats**: Ensure files are in widely accepted formats like PDF for documents, JPG for images, and MP4 for videos.
4. **Contact Technical Support**: If problems persist, provide them with:
    - **Screenshot of Error Message**: Helps in diagnosing the issue.
    - **Device and Browser Information**: Include details like browser version and operating system.

- - **Exact Time of Attempted Submission**: Facilitates log checks for errors.
  - **Example Email for Alternative Submission Method:**

    Subject: Technical Difficulty with Speaker Submission Form

    Dear [Name],

    I'm experiencing technical difficulties with the speaker submission form for [Event Name]. The system [specific issue] when I attempt to [specific action].

    Would it be possible to submit my materials via email or another alternative? I am eager to meet your [deadline date] deadline and have all materials prepared.

    Thank you for your assistance.

    Best regards,

    [Your Name]

5. **Prevention Strategies**
   - **Complete Applications in Text Editor**: Draft all application text in a word processor to avoid losing work if the browser or form fails.

- **Save Work Frequently**: Regularly save your progress if the system allows, or keep local backups.
- **Prepare Files in Multiple Formats**: Have different file formats ready in case one type is not accepted.
- **Test Uploads with Sample Files**: Try uploading smaller or different file types to identify potential issues early.
- **Begin Submission Well Before Deadline**: Allow ample time to address any unforeseen technical issues without rushing.

By following these strategies, you can minimize the impact of technical issues on your speaking application process and ensure your materials are submitted successfully and on time.

Troubleshooting Missed Application Deadlines

Missing a deadline for a speaking opportunity can be disappointing, but there are still ways to potentially salvage the situation. Here's a guide on how to address and prevent missed application deadlines.

Symptoms of Missing Deadlines

- **Deadline Passed Before Submission**: Realized the deadline after it had passed.

- **Late Discovery of Opportunity**: Found out about the event just as or after the deadline expired.
- **Technical Issues Prevented Timely Submission**: Encountered technical difficulties that delayed the submission process.

Solutions to Missed Deadlines

1. **Submit Anyway with a Professional Note:**
- **Email Example:**

Subject: Late Speaker Submission - [Your Name]

Dear Selection Committee,

I recently discovered your call for speakers for [Event Name] and realized the deadline was on [date]. If you are still reviewing submissions, I would be grateful for the opportunity to be considered.

My presentation, "[Title]," directly addresses [key challenge] and offers [unique approach], which I believe would greatly benefit your audience. Attached are all required materials. I understand if the timing may prevent my consideration this time.

Regardless of your decision, I would appreciate being added to your contact list for any future opportunities.

Thank you for considering my late submission.

Sincerely,

[Your Name]

2. **Contact the Organizer Personally**: Explain your circumstances clearly and professionally, which may lead them to consider your application or keep you in mind for future opportunities.
3. **Ask to Be Considered as a Backup Speaker**: Offer to be available should any confirmed speakers have to cancel.
4. **Request Consideration for Future Events**: Express your interest in future opportunities and ask to be kept informed.

Prevention Strategies

- **Calendar Alerts for Deadlines**: Set reminders well in advance of the actual deadlines.
- **Personal Deadlines**: Aim to submit applications at least one week before the actual deadline to avoid last-minute issues.
- **Speaking Opportunity Tracking System**: Maintain a system to manage application dates, submission statuses, and follow-up tasks.

- **Industry Newsletters**: Subscribe to relevant newsletters that announce and remind about speaking opportunities.

By implementing these strategies, you can manage and mitigate the effects of missing a deadline. Building a proactive approach and maintaining organized tracking can help ensure that future opportunities are not missed and can even enhance your professional reputation through timely and considerate communication.

Troubleshooting Vague Response Feedback

Dealing with vague feedback can be frustrating for speakers seeking to improve their applications for future opportunities. Here's how to professionally seek constructive feedback and enhance your approach to increase success in future applications.

Symptoms of Vague Rejection Feedback

- **Generic Rejection Notice**: Received a standard template without specific details.
- **No Specific Reason for Non-selection**: Unclear why the application was not successful.

- **Uncertainty About Improving Future Submissions**: Lack of information impedes ability to improve.

Solutions to Vague Rejection Feedback

1. **Send a Professional Request for Feedback**:
- **Email Example**:

Subject: Thank You and Request for Feedback

Dear [Name],

Thank you for considering my proposal for [Event Name]. Although I was not selected this time, I am committed to improving and would greatly appreciate any specific feedback you could provide. This would help me understand your selection criteria better and strengthen my future submissions.

Could you please share insights on:

- Areas where my proposal could be improved?

- Topics that might better align with your audience's interests?

- Presentation elements that did not meet your event's needs?

Your feedback is invaluable, and I am eager to apply it to enhance my contributions to your future events.

Thank you for your time and consideration.

Best regards,

[Your Name]

2. **Analyze Successful Speakers**:
    - Review profiles and topics of selected speakers to identify patterns or elements that might have influenced their selection when applicable.
3. **Attend the Event**:
    - If feasible, attend the event to gain insights into the type of content and presentation styles that resonate with the audience and selection committee.
4. **Connect with Selected Speakers**:
    - Reach out to speakers who were selected to learn about their proposals and presentation approaches.
5. **Offer to Serve on Selection Committees**:
    - Involvement in selection committees for similar events can provide insights into the decision-making process and criteria.

Prevention Strategies

- **Research Past Selected Presentations**: Study previous years' programs to understand the type of topics and presentation styles that have been successful.
- **Network with Event Planners**: Build relationships with event planners to learn insights about their priorities and preferences.
- **Get Proposal Feedback from Colleagues**: Have peers review your proposal to catch potential weaknesses, before submitting.
- **Study Event Programs**: Analyze the event's themes, goals, and previous successful topics to tailor your submissions accordingly.

Implementing these strategies can significantly improve your understanding of rejection reasons and help refine your approach. Increase your understanding of the event's needs to ensure better alignment with event expectations to enhance your chances of future acceptance.

For speakers frequently applying to various events, managing login credentials for multiple application portals can become complex and error-prone. Here's a way to manage login details to ensure smoother access and reduce issues.

Symptoms of Login Credential Management Issues

- **Lost Passwords:** Inability to recall or find passwords for application portals
- **Multiple Accounts Created Accidentally:** Duplicate accounts created due to forgotten logins
- **Uncertainty About Previous Application Status:** Lost track of applications due to login issues

Solutions for Managing Login Credentials

1. **Use a Standardized Login Formula:**
   - **Username:** Always use your professional email address.
   - **Password Base:** Create a base password combined with an identifier for each platform.
     - **Example:** MyPassword2025_EventX

Prevention Strategies

- **Use Password Manager Software:** Automates password storage and retrieval, reducing the risk of lost or forgotten credentials.
- **Create Standardized Naming Convention:** Helps in remembering and managing passwords without needing to write them down.

- **Document All Portal Access Information:** Keeps a secure record of all login details, including usernames, passwords, and the purposes of each portal.
- **Test Logins Periodically:** Regularly check access to important portals, especially prior to important deadlines.
- **Use "Forgot Password" Function Before Creating Duplicate Accounts:** Always attempt to recover an existing account before starting a new one.

By implementing these strategies, you can minimize disruptions caused by login issues, maintain security, and streamline your application process for speaking opportunities. Efficient credential management not only saves time but also reduces stress.

Appendix B: Sample Topic Titles and Descriptions

Crafting compelling topic titles and descriptions is not just about drawing attention. A clear topic title makes a promise to your audience about the value they will receive. This appendix serves as a guide to develop effective and engaging titles and descriptions tailored to various industries and speaking formats. Here, you'll find examples that illustrate how to communicate the essence of your presentation succinctly and persuasively, ensuring that both event planners and attendees see the immediate relevance and potential impact of your sessions.

These topics are designed to cater to the current needs of your target audience.

Leadership and Management Topics

Title 1: "Lead Out Loud: Authentic Leadership in Challenging Times"

- **Description**: This keynote delivers practical strategies for leaders facing organizational changes. By exploring five core practices of resilient leadership: trust-building, enhanced communication, strategic protocol implementation, resistance management, and accountability systems. Leaders are equipped to uphold team cohesion and productivity. The session is interactive, allowing leaders to apply these strategies directly to their current challenges, ensuring they leave with actionable insights that can be immediately implemented in their organizations.

Title 2: "The Feedback Factor: Transforming Performance Through Constructive Conversations"

- **Description**: Effective feedback is critical in today's fast-paced work environments. This workshop introduces the CLEAR method: Concise, Logical, Empathic, Actionable, and Respectful. which transforms feedback delivery from potentially demoralizing to motivating. Through practical exercises, role-play, and coaching, managers will learn how to structure feedback to encourage performance improvement and maintain healthy team relationships. Participants will gain valuable tools and templates to aid in these conversations, along with a 30-day plan to integrate these practices into their management routines.

Title 3: "Decision Architecture: Building Frameworks for Strategic Clarity"

- **Description**: Addressing decision fatigue, this presentation teaches executives how to optimize decision-making processes within their organizations. It introduces decision architecture—a strategic approach to designing decision-making systems that streamline processes and enhance team alignment. Using insights from behavioral economics and organizational psychology, participants will learn to classify decision types, delegate effectively, and construct decision matrices. The application of these frameworks is demonstrated through case studies from Fortune 500 companies, showcasing significant reductions in meeting times and faster project implementations.

Each of these presentations is tailored to provide leaders and managers with the knowledge and tools they need to excel in today's challenging professional environments. They are designed to inform and to transform, with a strong focus on practical application and immediate impact.

Communication and Presentation Skills

Title: "Communication with Less Confrontation: Managing Difficult Conversations with Confidence"

- **Description**: Navigate the minefield of difficult workplace conversations with the neuroscience-backed PAUSE method (Prepare, Acknowledge, Understand, Specify, Engage). This session teaches techniques to transform confrontations into productive dialogues, with practice sessions for de-escalation and developing scripts for sensitive issues. Attendees gain the confidence to tackle challenging interactions while preserving professional relationships.

Title: "Amplify Your Presentations: From Information Sharing to Audience Transformation"

- **Description**: Elevate your presentation skills beyond mere content delivery. Learn storytelling, visual design, vocal variety, and physical presence to captivate and transform your audience. This workshop includes a record-review-refine cycle with personalized coaching, helping participants refine their style, with takeaway tools like recorded practices and a custom enhancement plan to ensure ongoing improvement.

Title: "Virtual Impact: Commanding Presence in Digital Environments"

- **Description**: Master the art of virtual communication to make a genuine impact in digital meetings and presentations. Discover how to optimize your digital presence, leverage technology, and engage effectively online. This session covers virtual platform features, adapting non-verbal cues for the camera, and maintaining audience attention, with hands-on exercises and feedback to immediately improve online effectiveness.

These topics address current professional challenges and also equip participants with immediate and actionable skills. These topics make them attractive messages for their events.

Personal Development and Resilience

Title 1: "Resilience Reset: Thriving Through Change and Challenge"

- **Description**: Unveil the crucial components of resilience in an era defined by unpredictability. This session explores five key resilience dimensions: physical, mental, emotional, social, and purposeful. Attendees will engage in interactive assessments and reflective exercises to understand their resilience patterns and learn strategies to bolster each dimension to prevent burnout. This actionable framework helps participants craft a personalized resilience blueprint, empowering them to thrive amid adversity.

Title 2: "The Productivity Code: Achieving More While Working Less"

- **Description**: Break free from the cycle of being 'busy but unproductive' with strategies rooted in the neuropsychology of performance. The session introduces the FOCAL method (Filter, Optimize, Concentrate, Automate, Liberate), teaching participants how to effectively manage their attention, energy, and time. Attendees will partake in hands-on exercises to build a bespoke productivity system, transforming overwhelming workloads into streamlined, output-driven processes. This transformative approach shifts focus from traditional time management to effective attention management.

Title 3: "Purposeful Innovation: Creating Value Through Strategic Creativity"

- **Description**: Address the imperative for consistent innovation within modern organizational contexts. This session unpacks the Innovation Pipeline methodology, guiding participants through the stages of identifying opportunities, brainstorming solutions, evaluating ideas, and implementing them effectively. Through collaborative exercises and case study analysis, attendees will gain hands-on experience in applying these strategies to current organizational challenges. Thus, equipping them with the skills to transform spontaneous ideas into strategic innovations.

Each of these topics provides deep insights into personal and professional growth. They also equip attendees with actionable tools and techniques for immediate application. These topics are attractive for personal development seminars, corporate training sessions, and leadership conferences.

Healthcare

Title: "The Empathy Advantage: Enhancing Patient Experience Through Communication Excellence"

- **Description**: Dive into the critical role of empathy in healthcare to significantly enhance patient experiences. This session introduces the CARE protocol: Connect, Attend, Respond, and Empower. CARE is designed to increase patient satisfaction scores. These strategies bolster adherence to treatments and decrease complaints. The presentation combines research-backed approaches with practical exercises, enabling participants to apply these skills in daily interactions to create impactful, positive outcomes in healthcare settings.

Technology

Title: "Human-Centered Development: Creating Technology That People Want to Use"

- **Description**: This session focuses on aligning technological developments with user needs to ensure successful product adoption. It offers practical approaches for integrating human factors into the development process, from user research to solution validation. Technology professionals will gain insights into user-centered design principles that streamline development cycles and enhance user satisfaction. The session includes case studies that illustrate successful applications of these strategies, providing a clear path from technical expertise to market success.

Education

Title: "Beyond Content Mastery: Preparing Students for an Uncertain Future"

- **Description**: Prepare students for a dynamic and unpredictable future with the ADAPT methodology: Agency, Digital literacy, Analysis, People skills, Transfer. This innovative approach equips educators with strategies to develop critical, future-ready skills that go beyond traditional content mastery. The session provides tools for integrating these skills into existing curricula, enhancing student engagement, and ensuring that education is a robust foundation for lifelong learning and adaptability.

Financial Services

Title: "The Trust Equation: Building Client Relationships in an Age of Skepticism"

- **Description**: Uncover the foundational elements of building and maintaining client trust in the financial services industry. This presentation delves into the Trust Equation, exploring its four components: Credibility, Reliability, Intimacy, Self-Orientation, and how they influence client relationships and business success. Financial professionals will learn how to apply these principles through interactive examples and exercises designed to transform client interactions into opportunities for deepening trust and enhancing business outcomes.

These descriptions aim to provide a comprehensive understanding of the topic's relevance and value to the specific industry. They encourage higher engagement levels from the target audience and foster a deep connection with the content presented.

Customization Examples for "Communication with Less Confrontation"

1. **Healthcare**

    - **Title**: "Communication with Less Confrontation: Managing Difficult Conversations in Patient Care"
    - **Focus**: Enhances healthcare professionals' ability to manage emotionally charged conversations with patients and family members, emphasizing empathy and clear communication to improve patient outcomes.

2. **Education**

    - **Title**: "Communication with Less Confrontation: Navigating Challenging Conversations in Academic Settings"
    - **Focus**: Equips educators with strategies to handle difficult discussions with students, parents, and colleagues, fostering a supportive and understanding educational environment.

3. **Technology**

    - **Title**: "Communication with Less Confrontation: Resolving Technical Disagreements Without Derailing Projects"
    - **Focus**: Aids tech professionals in handling disputes over project directions or technical decisions, ensuring collaborative problem-solving and innovation continuity.

4. **Financial Services**

    - **Title**: "Communication with Less Confrontation: Delivering Difficult Financial News With Clarity and Empathy"
    - **Focus**: Prepares financial advisors and bank personnel to deliver tough news to clients about investments or financial health, emphasizing transparency and sensitivity.

Customization Examples for "Leading Through Change"

1. **Healthcare**

    - **Title**: "Leading Through Change: Maintaining Quality Care During Healthcare Transformation"
    - **Focus**: Supports healthcare leaders in managing transitions such as policy shifts, technological upgrades, or organizational restructuring while maintaining high standards of patient care.

2. **Manufacturing**

    - **Title:** "Leading Through Change: Guiding Production Teams Through Technological Transitions"
    - **Focus:** Focuses on assisting managers in the manufacturing sector to lead their teams effectively through the integration of new technologies and methods.

3. **Retail**

    - **Title:** "Leading Through Change: Adapting Store Operations to Evolving Consumer Behaviors"
    - **Focus:** Helps retail managers navigate the shifting landscape of consumer expectations and shopping behaviors, ensuring agile and responsive store operations.

4. **Non-Profit**

    - **Title:** "Leading Through Change: Sustaining Mission Impact During Funding and Regulatory Shifts"

- **Focus**: Guides non-profit leaders through the challenges of adapting to changes in funding sources, regulatory environments, and community needs, ensuring that the organization's mission remains impactful.

These customized versions make the topics more relevant to the specific audiences. They also increase the value of the presentations by directly addressing the concerns and environments of those sectors.

Format Variations for "The Innovation Imperative"

1. **Keynote Version**

   - **Title**: "The Innovation Imperative: Staying Relevant in a Rapidly Changing Market"
   - **Duration**: 45-60 minutes
   - **Description**: This keynote inspires and equips participants with insights into how innovation shapes industry leaders and laggards. It combines motivational elements with actionable strategies, making it ideal for a broad audience at conferences or company-wide events. The focus on market disruptions and

adaptability resonates with senior executives and decision-makers concerned with strategic direction.

2. **Workshop Version**

    - **Title**: "The Innovation Implementation Lab: Turning Ideas into Organizational Impact"
    - **Duration**: 3-4 hours
    - **Description**: This workshop format is deeply interactive, suitable for smaller groups such as department teams or leadership retreats. It allows participants to dive into the specifics of their organizational challenges and emerge with concrete plans, making it highly practical and immediately applicable. The collaborative environment fosters teamwork and enhances problem-solving skills within the context of real business scenarios.

3. **Virtual Training Version**

    - **Title**: "Innovation Essentials: Building Creative Capability in Distributed Teams"
    - **Duration**: 90 minutes, online

- **Description**: Tailored for remote teams, this virtual training session addresses the nuances of fostering innovation in a non-traditional work environment. It is perfect for organizations with geographically dispersed teams or those adopting permanent remote work policies. The use of digital tools and techniques for remote collaboration ensures that participants can continue to innovate effectively, regardless of physical location.

These variations demonstrate a strategic approach to content delivery. This also ensures that the topic is relevant to the audience's immediate needs. Each version serves a distinct purpose, from sparking high-level strategic thinking in a keynote to facilitating detailed operational planning in a workshop, to adapting practices for remote environments in virtual training. This flexibility in delivery maximizes the speaker's reach and impact, catering to diverse professional settings and learning styles.

These themed event examples showcase how speakers can tailor their presentations to fit specific conference themes, ensuring their content resonates deeply with the event's overarching goals and audience expectations:

1. **Conference Theme: "Building Bridges"**

   - **Title Adaptation**: "Spanning the Gap: Building Communication Bridges Across Organizational Divides"
   - **Description**: This presentation addresses the crucial role of effective communication in bridging organizational silos and fostering collaboration across departments. It provides participants with practical tools and strategies to enhance interdepartmental communication, thereby strengthening organizational coherence and enhancing overall business performance. Ideal for industries experiencing rapid growth or restructuring, where communication between new or merging teams is essential.

2. **Conference Theme: "Future Forward"**

   - **Title Adaptation**: "The Resilience Roadmap: Future-Proofing Your Team for Tomorrow's Challenges"
   - **Description**: Focused on preparing teams for future challenges, this presentation delves into developing resilience and adaptability in the

workforce. It covers anticipating potential industry shifts, adopting new technologies, and cultivating a culture that embraces change. Suitable for industries facing digital transformation or disruptive market forces, this talk helps leaders and teams to survive and thrive in the face of future uncertainties.

3. **Conference Theme: "Reaching New Heights"**

    - **Title Adaptation**: "The Altitude Advantage: Elevating Performance Through Strategic Focus"
    - **Description**: This session explores how organizations can achieve peak performance by honing their strategic focus. It discusses setting precise goals, aligning team efforts with organizational vision, and leveraging core competencies to surpass competitors. Particularly fitting for sales conferences or corporate retreats, the presentation motivates and equips teams to reach higher levels of achievement through targeted actions and sustained commitment.

Each adaptation aligns with the conference theme and enriches it by adding depth and actionable insights. These adaptations help ensure that the presentations are not only informative but also memorable.

* * *

TITLE TRANSFORMATION EXAMPLES:

These title transformation examples effectively elevate the appeal and specificity of generic topics, making them more intriguing and relevant to potential audiences. Here's a closer look at how each transformation enhances the original titles:

1. **Original**: "Improving Team Communication"
    - **Transformed**: "Beyond the Meeting: Transforming Team Communication for Breakthrough Results"
    - **Enhancement**: This new title suggests a comprehensive approach that extends beyond traditional settings, like meetings, implying innovative strategies that achieve significant improvements in team dynamics and outcomes. It promises not just improvement but transformation.

2. **Original**: "Handling Difficult Customers"
   - **Transformed**: "The Opportunity in Opposition: Converting Difficult Customer Interactions into Loyalty-Building Moments"
   - **Enhancement**: The transformation shifts the focus from a defensive posture ("handling") to an opportunistic strategy. It reframes difficult interactions as chances to build customer loyalty, appealing to business professionals by suggesting a proactive and positive approach to common challenges in customer service.

3. **Original**: "Work-Life Balance"
   - **Transformed**: "The Integration Equation: Designing a Harmonious Life-Work Blend in a Boundary-Blurred World"
   - **Enhancement**: This new title recognizes the modern challenges of blurred boundaries between personal and professional life, offering a sophisticated and tailored solution. It moves away from the often-discussed concept of balance towards a more dynamic

integration, suggesting a methodical and personalized approach to achieving harmony in today's demanding world.

These transformed titles are likely to attract more attention and interest at conferences and seminars. Positioning these talks is valuable and essential for contemporary professionals facing common workplace challenges. They promise actionable insights and novel perspectives that go beyond standard advice, making each session a must-attend for targeted attendees.

* * *

Creating compelling titles and descriptions for your speaking topics is crucial for capturing the attention of event planners and potential attendees. Here's a guide to help you craft titles and descriptions that stand out:

Title Formation Formula

1. **Start with a compelling phrase or metaphor**: Choose words that grab attention and provoke curiosity while relating to the core message.
2. **Follow with a clarifying subtitle that explains the benefit**: This adds context and

communicates the direct benefits or value of the presentation to the audience.

Example:

- **Title**: "The Innovation Engine: Igniting Creativity for Sustained Growth"
    - **Phrase/Metaphor**: "The Innovation Engine"
    - **Clarifying Subtitle**: "Igniting Creativity for Sustained Growth"

Description Structure

1. **Opening statement**: Identify the problem or opportunity your session addresses.
2. **Methodology or approach**: Describe the unique angle or method you will use to tackle the topic.
3. **Specific skills or knowledge**: Outline the content that will be covered.
4. **Implementation methods**: Explain how attendees can apply what they learn in their professional or personal lives.
5. **Tangible takeaways**: List any tools, handouts, or resources you will provide.
6. **Expected outcomes**: Highlight the potential changes or improvements attendees can expect.

Example:

- **Title**: "The Innovation Engine: Igniting Creativity for Sustained Growth"
- **Description:** "In today's fast-paced markets, sustained growth relies heavily on a company's ability to innovate continuously. This presentation dives into the dual engines of creativity and systematic innovation. Attendees will learn to harness creative thinking techniques that fuel innovation and to implement a systematic approach to integrate these techniques within their teams. Through real-world examples and interactive exercises, participants will apply these techniques in session to generate actionable ideas. Participants will leave with a creativity toolkit that includes idea generation templates and a roadmap for establishing an innovation pipeline in their organizations. You'll be equipped to kickstart your innovation journey, leading to increased competitiveness and growth."

- **Here's a breakdown of what's above**:
    - **Opening Statement**: "In today's fast-paced markets, sustained growth relies heavily on a company's ability to innovate continuously."

- **Methodology**: "This presentation dives into the dual engines of creativity and systematic innovation."
- **Specific Skills**: "Attendees will learn to harness creative thinking techniques that fuel innovation and to implement a systematic approach to integrate these techniques within their teams."
- **Implementation Methods**: "Through real-world examples and interactive exercises, participants will apply these techniques in session to generate actionable ideas."
- **Tangible Takeaways**: "Participants will leave with a creativity toolkit that includes idea generation templates and a roadmap for establishing an innovation pipeline in their organizations."
- **Expected Outcomes**: "You'll be equipped to kickstart your innovation journey, leading to increased competitiveness and growth."

Key Elements to Include

- **Specific Audience Identification**: Modify your language and content to resonate with the exact demographic attending.

- **Concrete Benefits and Outcomes**: Articulate what content will be shared in your presentation.
- **Credibility Indicators**: Include mentions of relevant research, case studies, your experience, or notable past presentations.
- **Interactive Components**: Highlight any interactive elements like Q&A, workshops, live polls, or hands-on segments.
- **Practical Application Emphasis**: Focus on how the content can be practically applied in the attendees' professional or personal lives.
- **Unique Approach or Methodology**: Differentiate your presentation by describing what makes your approach unique.

By following these guidelines, you can create titles and descriptions that draw attention and communicate the value.

Appendix C: Learning Objectives Template

Learning objectives are indeed pivotal. They provide a clear framework for the content and help the audience understand what information will be covered. Here's a breakdown of how to construct these objectives:

Structuring Effective Learning Objectives

1. **Start with a Strong Action Verb**: Choose a verb that conveys the level of learning expected, such as "analyze," "design," "construct," or "evaluate." These verbs set clear expectations for the activities in which the audience will engage.

2. **Specify the Knowledge or Skill**: State the content that will be shared and the skills that will be demonstrated. This should be a continuation of the action verb and provide a clear focus on the subject matter.

3. **Application Context**: Indicate how the participants will be able to apply the knowledge or skills. This ties the learning back to their

professional or personal life, providing context and relevance.

Short Examples of Learning Objectives

- **Analyze** customer data to **develop** targeted marketing strategies that increase engagement.
- **Design** and **implement** a risk management plan that **minimizes** potential disruptions to project timelines and schedules.
- **Evaluate** different leadership styles to **identify** the most effective approach for managing diverse teams.

Detailed Examples:

- **Implement three conflict resolution techniques in team discussions**: This objective is excellent for a workshop aimed at enhancing team collaboration. It's actionable and provides clear outcomes that can be observed and measured during and after the session.

- **Identify five warning signs of employee disengagement**: Perfect for a management training session, this objective focuses on increasing managers' awareness and ability to proactively address team issues, contributing to better management and retention strategies.

- **Apply the CLEAR feedback model in performance reviews**: Ideal for HR professionals and team leaders, this objective equips participants with a structured method to deliver constructive and effective feedback, which can improve communication and performance within the team.

Why These Components Matter

- **Clarity and Direction**: Well-defined objectives help keep your presentation focused and organized. They ensure that every part of your session is aligned towards a specific goal.
- **Audience Engagement**: By knowing what to expect, participants are more likely to be engaged as they can see the direct benefits of attending.
- **Event Planner Confidence**: Clear objectives show event planners that you understand your audience and are prepared to deliver meaningful content. This makes you a more appealing choice for speaking opportunities as it reduces the perceived risk of your session not meeting attendee expectations.

Utilizing Learning Objectives

When used effectively, learning objectives can profoundly impact the effectiveness of your presentations. They are formalities and are integral in guiding the development of your content. Always revisit your objectives throughout the preparation process to ensure they remain relevant and aligned with your overall session goals.

Learning Objective Formula

Tips for Using This Formula Effectively:

- **Align with Audience Needs**: Make sure the objectives are relevant to the specific needs and challenges of your audience. Customization increases engagement and applicability.

- **Ensure Measurability**: Objectives should be crafted in a way that allows you to measure whether they have been achieved. This could be through direct observation, feedback, or follow-up assessments.

- **Be Concise and Clear**: While detail is important, clarity and conciseness should not be sacrificed. Learners should be able to quickly grasp what they are expected to learn and why it matters.

By adhering to this structured approach, you ensure that your educational content is both effective and focused, providing clear benefits to your audience and meeting the expectations of event planners and stakeholders.

Action Verb Bank by Learning Level

1. Knowledge/Remember

- *Purpose*: To recall or remember information without necessarily understanding it.
- *Verbs*: Analyze, cite, define, describe, identify, list, name, recognize, recall, relate, repeat, state.

Example Objectives:

- *State* the main principles of ethical leadership.
- *Recall* the steps in the scientific method.
- *Describe* the standard procedure for emergency evacuation.

2. Comprehension/Understanding

- *Purpose*: To understand the meaning of instructions and problems. Can explain ideas or concepts.

- **Verbs:** *Clarify, classify, compare, contrast, discuss, explain, interpret, outline, paraphrase, summarize, translate, understand.*

Example Objectives:

- ***Summarize*** *the key points of the new tax regulation.*
- ***Classify*** *different types of market segmentation strategies according to their characteristics.*
- ***Discuss*** *the implications of recent changes in data protection laws on the technology sector.*

3. Application/Apply

- **Purpose:** *To use information or concepts in new situations. This is the stage where theoretical learning converts into practical application.*
- **Verbs:** *Apply, calculate, demonstrate, develop, implement, modify, operate, organize, practice, schedule, solve, use.*

Example Objectives:

- ***Use*** *statistical software to analyze customer data.*
- ***Operate*** *a new piece of machinery following safety protocols.*
- ***Modify*** *an existing process to improve efficiency.*

4. Analysis/Analyze

- **Purpose**: To break information into parts to understand it better. This involves differentiating, organizing, and attributing the components.
- **Verbs**: Analyze, categorize, compare, contrast, differentiate, distinguish, examine, test.

Example Objectives:

- **Differentiate** between causation and correlation in data interpretation.
- **Examine** the financial outcomes of a business using ratio analysis.
- **Contrast** the leadership styles of transformational and transactional leaders.

By articulating learning objectives across these four categories, you tailor your educational content to cater to a broad spectrum of learning needs, facilitating a more impactful and comprehensive educational experience. Each level builds upon the previous one, creating a robust foundation for advanced understanding and application.

Appendix D: Professional Bio Templates

Introduction

Creating a compelling professional bio is crucial for us as speakers, as it showcases our expertise, credibility, and unique value. Below, you'll find guidelines and examples for crafting effective bios in three different lengths: short, standard, and full. These variations ensure you have a suitable bio for various platforms and purposes.

Short Bio (30 words)

- **Purpose**: Quickly grabs attention and conveys key qualifications
- **Use**: Social media profiles, event badges, quick introductions

Example: "Jane Doe, an award-winning financial analyst, revolutionizes investment strategies through data-driven methodologies. Featured in *Forbes* and *Bloomberg*."

Standard Bio (90 words)

- **Purpose**: Provides a snapshot of your background, what you do, and what makes you stand out.
- **Use**: Conference programs, speaker introductions, professional websites

Example: "Jane Doe leverages over 14 years of experience to offer groundbreaking investment insights. As a Certified Financial Analyst (CFA) with an MBA from Harvard, Jane has transformed financial portfolios by integrating advanced data analytics. Her innovative techniques have earned her features in *Forbes* and speaking spots at global finance conferences. Jane currently leads the R&D team at FinTech Innovations, developing tools that empower smarter investment decisions."

Full Bio (150 words)

- **Purpose**: Gives a detailed overview of the speaker's career, achievements, and areas of expertise.
- **Use**: Detailed program bios, personal websites, press releases

Example: "Jane Doe is a distinguished financial analyst and a thought leader in quantitative investment strategies, with over 14 years of field expertise. Holding an MBA from Harvard and a CFA certification, Jane's career is highlighted by her tenure at FinTech Innovations, where she spearheads the research and development department. Her pioneering work in utilizing machine learning to predict market trends has redefined traditional investing, making her a sought-after speaker at international finance conferences and a featured expert in *Forbes* and *Bloomberg*. Beyond her professional pursuits, Jane is passionate about mentoring young analysts and advocating for women in finance. She also contributes to 'Financial Literacy for All,' a nonprofit aimed at educating underserved communities."

Guidelines for Crafting Your Bio

1. **Tailor Your Bio**: Adjust your bio according to the audience and the purpose. Highlight aspects most relevant to your current speaking engagement or professional interaction.
2. **Update Regularly**: Keep your bio updated with your most recent achievements, positions, and qualifications.
3. **Focus on Value**: Emphasize how your work impacts your audience or field. Mention specific projects or roles and their outcomes.
4. **Include Credentials and Recognition**: Mention certifications, awards, or recognitions that elevate your professional standing.

5. **Third-Person Voice**: Write in the third person for a more formal and universally acceptable tone.

By following these templates and guidelines, you can create a professional bio that effectively communicates your expertise and unique contributions to potential clients, event planners, and your professional community.

Bio Structure Elements

Effective professional bios typically include these key elements:

1. **Professional Identity** - Who you are professionally
2. **Expertise/Specialization** - Your specific area of expertise
3. **Methodology/Approach** - Your unique methodology or approach
4. **Experience/Background** - Relevant experience and qualifications
5. **Accomplishments/Results** - Notable achievements and outcomes
6. **Audience Relevance** - How your work benefits your audience
7. **Personal Element** - Humanizing detail (primarily in longer versions)

8. **Call to Action** - Next steps for engagement (primarily in longer versions)

Not all elements appear in every bio version. Short bios focus on elements 1-3, standard bios incorporate elements 1-6, and full bios include all eight elements.

www.ingramcontent.com/pod-product-compliance
Lightning Source LLC
Chambersburg PA
CBHW071855290426
44110CB00013B/1152